Rhetorical Questions

Edwin
Black

Rhetorical Questions

Studies of
Public
Discourse

The University of
Chicago Press

Chicago and London

Edwin Black is professor of communication arts at the University of Wisconsin—Madison and the author of *Rhetorical Criticism: A Study in Method.*

The University of Chicago Press, Chicago 60637
The University of Chicago Press, Ltd., London
© 1992 by The University of Chicago
All rights reserved. Published 1992
Printed in the United States of America

01 00 99 98 97 96 95 94 93 92   5 4 3 2 1

ISBN (cloth): 0–226–05501–9

Library of Congress Cataloging-in-Publication Data

Black, Edwin
    Rhetorical questions : studies in public discourse / Edwin Black.
        p.   cm.
    Includes bibliographical references (p.   ) and index.
    1. Oratory.   2. Rhetoric.   3. Criticism.   I. Title.
    PN4096.B57   1992
    808.5'1—dc20   91–28534
                                                                            CIP

To Sharon

Contents

Acknowledgments

―――― *It is impossible to record the names of all those to whom I owe thanks. The list would have to include, among others, more than twenty years of graduate students and faculty colleagues who have participated in the Rhetoric Colloquium at the University of Wisconsin–Madison. At various times they patiently endured primitive versions of some of the paragraphs that follow, and I have profited from their sharp questioning.*

Among those who have given me help with particular portions of this book, I am especially grateful to Stephen Lucas, Hanns Hohmann, Emiko Ohnuki-Tierney, Vance Kepley, Jr., Fred Kauffeld, and Keith Yellin.

The University of Chicago Press, personified to me by senior editor John Tryneski, has been every bit as splendid as its reputation. And the Press's two anonymous reviewers provided careful and sympathetic readings of my manuscript for which I am deeply obliged.

Finally, I thank Tillie Black, whose serene companionship during my writing frenzy continuously reminded me of that luminous universe of value that extends beyond language.

This book is dedicated to Sharon Ruhly Black. The particulars of my indebtedness to her are shielded by the attorney-client relationship.

Madison, Wisconsin   E. B.
April 1991

Bibliographical Note

———— *The* Quarterly Journal of Speech *(May 1988) published an earlier version of chapter 2, "Secrecy and Disclosure as Rhetorical Forms."* Chapter 4, *"The Sentimental Style as Escapism," is based on an essay that appeared in* Form and Genre: Shaping Rhetorical Action *(1978), published by the Speech Communication Association. Chapter 6, "Ideological Justifications," appeared in the* Quarterly Journal of Speech *(May 1984). An earlier version of chapter 8, "The Mutability of Rhetoric," appeared in* Rhetoric in Transition *(1980), published by the Pennsylvania State University Press.*

Introduction:
Rhetoric as Critique

───── The pun is intended. A rhetorical question can be either an issue pertinent to the discipline of rhetoric or a kind of trope that propels form in one direction and substance in another. *Rhetorical Questions* participates in both senses. The book records some critical engagements with discourses that are on the boundary between literature and politics. And it records also, although less premeditatedly, a fascination with the tensions between form and substance that pervade those discourses. It is thus a volume of rhetorical criticism.

Rhetorical criticism, as a hermeneutical endeavor, exerts a chronic temptation to circularity, so that the most fastidious analysis may end simply by reaffirming the convictions with which it began. Often, the only question asked at the threshold of a rhetorical critique is a form of rhetorical question: Will I find confirmed in the discourse that I examine the presuppositions with which I examine it? The question, like a rhetorical question, has its answer already etched within it. A lens ground to a certain prescription will, of course, always refract in the same way, irrespective of the source of light.

The strain of these essays—another pun, entailing both their commonality and their author's *Kampf*—is the effort to confront rhetorical phenomena with real questions, to elicit information rather than confirmation from them, to elude the role of interrogative *schnorrer* that the asker of rhetorical questions plays. In that sense, then, the title of this book is the antipathy of its ambition.

An ordinary question—a *real* question—functions to elicit an answer. What will count as an answer to a question is defined with fair exactitude by our common agreements on relevance: agreements that help to constitute what we ordinarily regard as rationality (a term used here in full knowledge that it has become contested). A question is socially mandating. To ignore it is to risk giving offense. A question, asked in circumstances that will condone the asking, solicits a response that must be selected from a limited inventory of responses: an answer, an evasion, or a confession of ignorance.

A question may, of course, be used for an interpretive purpose. Insofar as a question is expressive, it can be construed by an auditor symptomatically, as evidence of what the asker knows or does not know; but drawing such an inference from a question does not repeal the question's social entailments.

A question becomes unequivocally rhetorical when it acquires the hue of benign deception: a declarative statement posing as an interrogative. It is no more deceptive than other ironies that feint in one direction and move in another, but it has abandoned the beckoning innocence of a real question— one that is seeking an answer rather than sponsoring one.

A rhetorical question is asked for the persuasive effect of its asking. It solicits assent to a proposition by a subtle shift of the burden of proof. It is a question whose form baits and whose substance hooks, a declaration that solicits assent to a claim by tickling the auditor's social obligation to respond to an interrogative.

A question is rhetorical if it is either so profound that answering it is obviously impossible, or so superficial that answering it is impossibly obvious. A rhetorical question uses the auditor's silence for its own confirmation. It may be the most miniature of iterated persuasive patterns.

That a declarative assertion clad in interrogative disguise is called a rhetorical question is germane to why the conception of criticism that is sustained in this book is rhetorical. The questions whose answers are sought here are real, not rhetorical, but the term "rhetorical criticism" refers here to a bilateral study. One aspect of it—the synthetic—is concerned with the relationships among ideas that constitute a system of belief. The other aspect—the analytic—is concerned with functional incongruities of the sort that the rhetorical question exemplifies: a form (interrogative) imperfectly matched to a substance (declarative). The same sort of mismatch occurs when public discourse is made to serve private motives: a theme that is inscribed, in one way or another, on all of the essays of this volume. To clarify the conception of rhetorical criticism that informs these essays, we should begin with its analytic aspect, and this we can best do comparatively.

I

Since the conclusion of World War II, there have been at least three intellectual movements, all occupied with the explication of texts, that are commensurable with rhetorical criticism, and that therefore may provide bearings for its location. These three movements are the New Criticism, General Semantics, and Deconstruction.

The first of these, the New Criticism, was an orientation to literature that dominated Anglo-American criticism for three decades, and that has left a substantial residue of allegiance among critics. The second critique, General Semantics, had considerable notoriety for a period, and is now as dead and gone as a theory can be. The third, Deconstruction, is a movement that has been more recently fashionable among literary theorists, and that still exerts a waning influence. The nature of rhetorical criticism as practiced in these pages may emerge with greater clarity in comparison with these three approaches to the interpretation of discourse.

Although it inspired a notable body of speculative work, the New Criticism has to be regarded as a nontheoretical perspective, especially in comparison with the other two critiques under scrutiny. It was much more clearly in the tradition of British empiricism than of continental theory, and it fixed tenaciously on the concrete text and its formal characteristics. The New Criticism, whose roots go back to influential publications by T. S. Eliot and I. A. Richards in the twenties and thirties, exalted ambiguity, condensation, and irony as literary values, all of which accentuate the multiplicity of simultaneous meanings that are possible to a text.

Deconstruction emphasizes the indefiniteness of the text— the elusiveness of its interpretation—but ends also by stressing the multiplicity of senses, especially contradictory ones, that can be associated with it. We have had, then, for over fifty years an important tendency in literary criticism to highlight the semantic plurality of texts. And the main difference between the New Criticism and Deconstruction is that where the New Criticism sought to discover multiple meanings that were coherent and reciprocally reinforcing, Deconstruction seeks multiple meanings that are discrepant and reciprocally sabotaging.

The New Criticism insistently focused on the autonomous text, celebrating its richness in ambiguity and irony, its capacity to layer meanings upon one another and to convey them all in a statement of organic complexity. By contrast, Deconstruction's putative discovery of the indefiniteness of texts attributes autonomy to the language rather than the text. To Deconstruction, ambiguity is not the product of a complex mastery of language; it is rather the manifestation of the language's refusal to be mastered, of its independence of regulation.

Because in Deconstruction there is always a disparity between the conscious intention of the author and the actual function of the text, a text is like Frankenstein's monster: it acquires a life of its own that is, from the standpoint of its creator, both independent and malevolent. But that analogy is sharply limited, for the relationship between creator and created is not clouded in Mary Shelley's story. There it is clear that Dr. Frankenstein preceded his monster. The language, however, preceded Mrs. Shelley, and a deconstructionist reading of her novel would disclose the secret codicils that it denyingly affirms and affirmingly denies. She, like every writer before and after her, was born into a language that betrays her effort to control it.

Deconstruction can be interpreted as an exploration of hypocrisy in literature. Its adherents are not engaged in any pious quest for sincerity, but they do relish the infidelities of discourse. That is not to say that the movement endorses hypocrisy. It merely savors it. And that indiscretion is the inevitable by-product of a project that sees its mission as the exposure of literature's chronic misrepresentation.

The moral sensibility of Deconstruction bears comparison to the moral sensibility of *Consumer Reports*. Both seek to uncover the disparity between claims and intentions; both cultivate in their clients a suspicion of reflexive testimony; both test the objects of their diagnosis by subjecting them to extreme stress. The difference between them is that *Consumer Reports* professes for itself nothing loftier than a simple honesty, but to Deconstruction, honesty is never simple. Its proponents are, as college debaters used to say, "significantly silent" about its own integrity as a theory.

Deconstruction has so corrosive a view of language that its own survival is a continual embarrassment. Deconstruction is, after all, formulated in no medium other than the language that it encourages us to mistrust, and its implicit claims to exemption from its own indictment of that language are based, rather awkwardly, on faith.

If there is to be any theoretical salvation of Deconstruction, it may be contained in a fifty-year-old formulation by Lionel Trilling, a critic whose work is hopelessly passé and untheoretical by deconstructive standards. Trilling wrote, "A culture is not a flow, nor even a confluence; the form of its existence is struggle, or at least debate—it is nothing if not a dialectic. And in any culture there are likely to be certain artists who contain a large part of the dialectic within themselves, their meaning and power lying in their contradictions; they contain within themselves, it may be said, the very essence of the culture, and the sign of this is that they do not submit to serve the ends of any one ideological group or tendency."[1]

"Culture," in this view, is a maze of conflicting ideas, mutating in their relations over time, the whole held together only by a set of rules and practices that make the perpetuation of the dialectic possible. These rules and practices, for the most part, bear on the social contract and effectuate communication. Thus, the claim that a specific value is culturally determined is usually, at best, a half-truth because its opposites can also be found to have voices in the dialectic. For every hero produced by Western culture, there is a villain; for every dogmatic absolute, there is a diffident relativism; for every certitude, there is a doubt; for every affirmation, a denial. It does not do to be too facile about the characteristics of any complex culture—European, American, hyphenated American, or any other.

A generous, perhaps even charitable, interpretation of Deconstruction's insistence on the contradictory character of discourse would be that such a view simply apprehends literary works as microcosms of their cultural matrices. Deconstruction would thus be construed as taking seriously—maybe even beyond seriously, to obsessively—our conventional piety, embodied in the Whorf hypothesis, that language will reflect cultural values. And naturally—or in this context I should say unnaturally, for it is not nature but art that we are considering—the tensions, contradictions, distortions, hypocrisies, illusions, instabilities, and incompatibilities that mark the life of a culture will mark also and ineluctably the linguistic manifestations of that culture. This interpretation of Deconstruction, however, may domesticate a movement that its surviving adherents would prefer be left fractious.

An earlier movement, equivalent to Deconstruction in its ponderousness if not in its pedigree, was General Semantics. Its guru was one Count Alfred Korzybski, its scripture was entitled *Science and Sanity*, and forty years ago, its disciples were a presence in some of our universities.

The therapeutic essence of General Semantics was expressed in the epiphany that cow_1 was not the same as cow_2. We would not, of course, have to be reminded that cows are different from one another if they did not appear to be alike. So there again was an intellectual movement whose fugitive moment of celebrity was based on the imposture of appearance.

It is also significant that the corrective response of General Semantics to the perfidious snares of common speech took the form of a radical nominalism, a refusal to concede that categorical designations signified realities. Secure in the empirically earned conviction that the identity of each object is unique, semanticists did not rush to consign to any object, excepting collective nouns, the attributes of another object that happened to be called by the same name. General Semantics observed the human misery produced by perseveration, the disasters of refusing to adapt to singularity. It counseled the fresh, the unprejudiced discovery of each object of experience at each moment of perception.

No chair ever collapsed beneath the weight of a general semanticist. Their bottoms were lowered with the caution of the truly enlightened. Thus they may be distinguished from deconstructionists, whose bottoms are lowered indiscriminately.

Neither the New Criticism nor General Semantics nor Deconstruction is generic or historical. The New Criticism, in fact, arose as a reaction against literary history and genre studies, and was comprehended in the profession of literary criticism as antithetical to them. The essential interests of General Semantics and Deconstruction are not served by comparative studies, and although the New Criticism can accommodate comparative studies, the movement was not hospitable to them. These movements all, in different ways and to different degrees, are marked by nominalism: by the inclination to inspect the single object in preference to the class of objects, and to apprehend that object functionally rather than historically. That last characteristic—functionality—is the common ground that these three critiques share with rhetorical criticism.

We have, then, three movements, arbitrarily chosen, dedicated to explicating the complexities of meaning that are concealed and sometimes disfigured by ostensible significations. One of these movements—the New Criticism—celebrates the capacities of language, especially poetic language, to convey multifarious meanings in a distilled and unified way. The other two movements—General Semantics and Deconstruction—are more cautionary and censorious in their responses to the covert complexities of language. General Semantics sponsored a program of immunization against the snares and delusions of common speech. Deconstruction purports to disclose that the intrinsic instability of meaning muddles the relations between the text and its audience and subverts authorial intentions. All three critiques are focused on the discrepancies between appearance and reality. All three critiques prefer reality, although it is hard to imagine anyone believing that they are equally adept at discovering it.

The two critiques that have been principally concerned with fictive literature—the New Criticism and Deconstruction—diverge in their attitudes toward the recondite intricacies that they seek to disclose. The New Criticism sponsors the propitious revelation that some authors are more ingenious and resourceful than they appear. Deconstruction sponsors the disenchanting revelation that most authors are less magisterial and consistent than they appear. The critique that was principally concerned with literal uses of language—General Semantics—sponsors the revelation that dangerous sources of lunacy and confusion are in common speech. The New Criticism and Deconstruction issue finally in attitudes toward literature. General Semantics issues finally in prescriptions governing behavior.

To become a New Critic is to apprehend a text as, in the words of Walter Jackson Bate, "organic because it is *independent*, with a virtually self-sufficient life of its own."[2] To become a deconstructionist is to apprehend what the benighted call a text as indefinite, incoherent, and heterogeneous. To become a general semanticist is to abjure induction and to move from one moment to the next as if each moment were lived in its own singular world.

Although rhetorical criticism has in common with the three movements a functional orientation, rhetorical criticism is not committed to a nominalistic view of its subjects. If anything, the contrary is closer to the truth. Inasmuch as originality is not prized among rhetors as it is among litterateurs, there is an almost complacent conventionality in rhetorical practice, one that would be appalling to connoisseurs of literature. The rhetorical critic is driven by the nature of the critical object to comparative judgments and generic understandings.

Rhetoric-as-critique, then, is unique among these four critiques in having no defining or a priori commitment about the scope of its application. The rhetorical critic is free to view discourse historically, comparatively, generically, or isolatedly. These other three critiques, for different reasons, are not.

More important, it is not at all clear that rhetoric as such shares with the three critiques a fixation on the differences between appearance and reality. Insofar as a rhetor is hypocritical, the exploration of that hypocrisy could be a fruitful exercise in rhetorical criticism. But the speaker whose utterance and intention are perfectly coextensive—the rhetor, in short, who is completely sincere—may well be a subject of rhetorical criticism without presenting to the critic any disparity at all between appearance and reality.

Indeed, there is an important sense in which, insofar as rhetorical criticism is concerned, rhetors always are exactly as they appear. And that is because the subject of rhetorical criticism is appearance, mere appearance. We study nothing else except as dilettantes.

Even in the case of the hypocritical subject, if the hypocrisy itself is no part of the appearance—if, in sum, it is undetectable except by extrarhetorical evidence—then its exposure by a rhetorical critic is a gratuity. Textually undetectable hypocrisy is not pertinent to a rhetorical critique because it is not a rhetorical phenomenon. It is not woven into the texture of appearance.

Rhetorical criticism shares with psychoanalysis at least one fundamental conviction: For its purposes, no one ever lies. People can, of course, say things that they do not understand, or that they believe only temporarily, or even that they actively disbelieve at the moment of utterance. But those sorts of statements and misstatements are all material to the truths that rhetorical criticism seeks.

When Richard Nixon proclaimed to the nation during the Watergate scandal, "I'm not a crook," he was uttering truth to the rhetorical critic: truth about his representation of the issues attending Watergate, truth about his interpretation of his own motives, truth about the condition to which he had already fallen. Such statements are as informative as, often more informative than, the necessarily simple linguistic formulation that conforms wholly and faithfully to some raw datum of experience.

Rhetoric is a critique predicated on the premise that appearances have real consequences. In the cosmic opposition between noumena and phenomena, the data of rhetorical criticism are phenomena.

Rather than being centered in any disassociation between appearance and reality, the rhetorical study originates in the interstices between form and substance. Where form and substance fuse into indistinguishable homogeneity, there is no room for rhetorical inquiry. The statements "Two plus two equals four" and "It is raining outside" are impervious to rhetorical analysis. They represent a completely fulfilled amalgamation of form and substance. Neither statement offers even a scintilla of incoherence on which a rhetorically oriented interpretation can brace itself. But what if those two statements are changed to introduce the issue of appearance versus reality? What if the examples were "Two plus two equals five," and "It is raining outside" uttered when it was *not* raining outside? Does the falsity of the statements bring them within the discipline of rhetoric? The answer has to be that the false statements can no more be subjected to rhetorical criticism than the true ones. It is not the truth or falsity of statements that enables rhetorical criticism to illuminate them.

Rhetorical study becomes operative when there is a perceptible disparity between form and substance; when, in sum, language is used to convey more than the literal sense of a claim and a literal report of the evidence warranting it. That is why we do not have and cannot have rhetorical critiques of a prodigious body of discourses produced by the physical and biological sciences, despite the fact that those efforts are typically argumentative in structure.[3] Their formulary language unites form and substance into an indissoluble whole, leaving no room for even the most timorous rhetorical interpretation.

On rare occasions the incongruity that triggers rhetorical interest originates in an intentional misrepresentation, a blatant effort to divorce appearance from reality. More often, the source is a less culpable human imperfection: the demands of tact, for example, or the extranecessitous effort to please, to be approved, to be respected, to be remembered, to be taken seriously, to be believed. But whatever their origins, such tensions are a necessary condition for rhetorical criticism to occur.

People long have dreamed of a language so pure that no lie can be uttered in it, a language in which equivocation cannot be plausibly invested. In a sense, the highest achievements of poetry exhibit such capacities. There are poems so finely wrought in a language of such purity that the subtlest falsification would be detectable in them. At the other end of a continuum of nuanced perceptions, rhetorical criticism can be seen as a perspective on language that does not admit deception. The rhetorical critic is an omnivorous consumer of discourse, gleaning truths about motive, attitude, intention, and ambition from it all. The critic's only requirement is that the discourse be above a minimum threshold of complexity, that it have a density sufficient for it to be formally imperfect.

This consideration of rhetoric's relationship to the ancient diremption of appearance and reality would be incomplete without noting a related diremption, that of the fictive and the literal. In dealing with that bifurcation too, the animus of rhetorical criticism would be to focus not on the differences between the moieties, but on their commonalities of technique and effect. Rhetorical criticism, for example, would note the systemic similarities between the novel and the ideology—the fact that both are structured, that both are self-contained, that both have to be internally consistent to retain their plausibility, that both are based on acts of faith. Rhetorical criticism would note that the internal consistency of the novel and of the ideology is not distinctively logical, but that it is an internal consistency based on conventions of compatibility that are elaborated within the work itself.

The novel develops in the reader attitudes toward its own characters and events, so that its persuasion is reflexive; its persuasion of the reader concerns itself: its settings, its situations, its characters, and their relationships. However, because the novel continuously solicits moral judgments from the reader, it rehearses the reader in certain forms of moral judgment, and to the extent that its fictitious events or characters can be identified by the reader with real events or characters, the judgments that the novel encourages the reader to make can be said to be its immediate persuasive effect. If the reader identifies the novel's fictitious events or characters with real events or persons, and extends to them the moral judgments that the novel has rehearsed, that can be said to be the novel's residual persuasive effect.

The ideology, by contrast, purports to refer to the real world; it solicits a literal response. The immediate moral judgments of events or characters that the ideology induces have implications for action that are direct rather than analogous. Its events and characters are elaborated in a series of truth-claims.

One is invited to become a participant in an ideology—a character of the work. The same sort of surrender to a novel would flirt with lunacy; but because human contrivances are imperfect, there are rare occasions when a novel may be taken literally, when a *Werther* renders youthful angst unbearable, or an *Uncle Tom's Cabin* vivifies and consolidates a moral judgment. Conversely—and fortunately—there are frequent occasions when an ideology is viewed as fictitious.

The important point for our purposes is that novels and ideologies share important properties of structure and function. They are, therefore, amenable to common forms of analysis. They are distinguishable from one another principally in their media, and in the orientations to themselves that they solicit from their auditors.

Another development deserves mention in this connection. It is the increasing association of artistic creativity with subconscious activity, and the impact of that development on rhetorical studies. Insofar as an Aristotelian view of art as craftsmanship—"A habit of production in conscious accordance with a correct method"[4]—was regnant, only the deliberately willed could be considered within the province of an art, including the art of rhetoric. When, however, a Platonic view of artistic creativity as a species of unreason, finding its source in mysterious inspiration, was revived by the romantic movement, it became possible, even mandatory, to include within the domain of criticism the inadvertent, the accidental, the unwilled, the spontaneous, the uncalculated, the dreamed, the hallucinated. We now see them all as indispensable sources of artistic creation.

This modern dispensation, which shifted the meaning of "art" from process to object, has put us in a universe where our conscious and articulable selves are superficial symptoms of the unconscious, the unutterable, even the unthinkable. We routinely conceive of our will as transcending our knowledge of it.

One consequence to rhetorical criticism of this development, but not alone to rhetorical criticism, has been the extension of its province. Instead of the scope of rhetorical criticism being confined to the ratios between the rhetor's calculations and the discourse's effects, the way was opened to extend critical inquiry into two dimensions that were formerly closed. First, a discourse could be apprehended as expressive as well as instrumental. Public as it may be, calculated as it may be, the rhetorical discourse can still be seen as the symptom of its author, exhibiting more than the author intended, a transcript of reluctant testimony, an accidental confession. Second, the generic provenance of the discourse could be found in its structural and figural character more than in its subject or occasion. Those subtler analogies of discourses with one another more likely correspond to their allocations by the publics that they create. A speech, like a film or a play or a novel, is interpreted through its auditor's memory of comparable artifacts. Its meaning and effect will pivot on its alignments within the personal history of its audience. So comprehended, genre becomes a functional constituent of the rhetorical transaction.

II

We have been considering rhetorical criticism as an orientation to certain relations between discourse and its referents. There is another dimension to rhetorical criticism that also affects this book: a synthetic dimension. John Crowe

Ransom once usefully distinguished between the texture and the structure of poetry, and that same distinction, applied to prose, invites our attention now to the structural component of rhetorical criticism.

It is no accident that a consideration of rhetorical criticism should focus on bipolarities. Rhetorical activity is an order of experience that is permeated with oppositions. Every proposition that is treated rhetorically is contestable. Even in an epideictic circumstance, where pieties are being rehearsed, the central claims of discourse must be affirmed against the countervailing prospects of the decay or neglect or discredit of those claims. There is no rhetorical activity that does not represent a tension; no affirmation that is unattended by the possibility of denial. Rhetoric has an intrinsically disputatious character. And while I would not want to make too much of that, while I would not want to make that observation the ground of any critical technique, and certainly not the principle of any system, I must, in accounting for these essays, confess that I discover in them the elements of a program that I little suspected at the time of their composition. That program has two parts: One is an exploration of the actions and tensions of argumentative incompatibility, and the other is an exploration of its antonym—the nature of coherence, the reticulate character of beliefs that, when viewed comprehensively, constitute an ideology.

A book that was published twenty-five years ago, *Rhetorical Criticism: A Study in Method*, contained, near its end, a treatment of something that I called "argumentative incompatibility." That treatment was so brief as to be almost cryptic. The concept appears repeatedly in this volume, not explicitly as a theoretical formulation, but rather implicitly as a technique of analysis.

Propositions that appear in rhetorical transactions to be in conflict can be said to be incompatible. Incompatibility is not the same as contradiction because incompatible propositions can sometimes be resolved, but contradictions never can. One would be hard put to find contradictions that are rhetorically compatible, but it is easy to find incompatibilities that are not contradictory. Indeed, one of the tasks of political compromise is to accommodate incompatibilities, and that would not be possible if they were contradictory. Another reason for disassociating incompatibility from contradiction is that a given proposition may have—probably will have—more than one incompatibility, while a contradiction may consist simply of P and not-P.

Contradictions do not diminish; they abide in the timeless realm of logic; but rhetorical incompatibilities may be reconciled. Repeatedly in history, repeatedly in our own lifetimes, values and principles that a group finds antagonistic to their very existence come finally to be assimilated by them, and they live on. Sometimes their conversion is accomplished quickly by terror or seduction, sometimes slowly by the languid evaporation of their certitude—but however done, it is done.

The white South Carolinian of 1860 who regarded a civil society without the enslavement of black people as unthinkable, intolerable, lived to think it, to tolerate it, to accept it, maybe even, in time, to welcome it. The Marxist economy of the Soviet Union, whose tenets were once so exalted as to be buoyed on an ocean of blood, is disassembled in the face of its manifest ruin, and the once professed incompatibility between private profit and public good is not simply abandoned; its very opposite is embraced. The domesticity of women, which only recently was divinely ordained and integral to the natural order, withers throughout the West in unendurable embarrassment, confounded by principles of equity so persuasive that they move inexorably toward their own realization.

We live by affirming against negations, but we also live by adapting and yielding and changing. Rhetorical criticism is concerned with those mutable collisions; with the frictions between oppositional ideas, and, sometimes, with their reciprocal adaptation; with what is opposed to what, and with what is anathema to whom.

The language imposes reason on its users. Of course that does not mean that every sentence uttered or written makes sense. No reader of criticism can fail to be aware of the intellectual atrocities to whose commission language may be appropriated. Yet, however twisted, however choked, some rationality persists in human speech. That is because a noise totally devoid of reason would communicate nothing but its own idiot vacancy. To forgo reason entirely is also to forgo grammar and syntax, to forgo language itself.

It follows that anything any of us would be inclined even to call an ideology would necessarily display at least the shards of a rational order. Minimally, it will proffer justifications for its claims; it will have some account of its adversaries; it will display some connections among its leading ideas; it will speak itself in sentences. As Hofstadter has shown in his examination of the paranoid style, there are forms of ideological madness that even represent an excess of reason rather than a deficiency of it.[5]

The relations among the convictions constituting an ideology are those of compatibility. The display of one such conviction is a fallible sign of all the others. Fallible signs, of course, are matters of statistical probability. When a certain probability is reached that the possession of one belief—say, a belief in the efficacy of laetrile as a cure for cancer—will signal the possession of another, *logically unentailed* belief—say, a conviction that the National Institutes of Health and the American Medical Association conspire to suppress truth—then those two beliefs can be said to be rhetorically compatible; either of them paired with the contrary of the other would, to a particular public, be rhetorically incompatible; and the two together would likely be constituents of an ideology.

There are no formulary descriptions of rhetorical compatibility known to me. Each case of ideological commitment may—probably will—recapitulate a familiar structure, but its interstitial adhesions will be unique to it. The essays that follow are all, in one way or another, concerned with the relations among the ideas that mark an ideology or a rhetor. The theme of rhetorical compatibility attends them all.

III

Finally, I have been urged to address the relationship, if any, of the present volume to *Rhetorical Criticism: A*

Study in Method: a subject that I undertake with reluctance. The main burden of that earlier work, and, I think, its main effect as well, was to help create space. Rhetorical criticism was, prior to 1965, associated with a stifling creed of practice—one that allowed the critic little room for interpretive originality or unorthodox judgment. To some degree, the condition was attributable to a misreading of Herbert Wichelns's great essay, "The Literary Criticism of Oratory," and to some other degree of it was attributable simply to the excess of caution and deficiency of imagination that may have been responsible for the misreading of Wichelns in the first place. Whatever the reasons for the prevailing critical practice, *Rhetorical Criticism* was intended to attack it, and the book was so construed both by its detractors and its supporters.

Most of the pages of *Rhetorical Criticism* were occupied with refutation, and fewer with affirmative assertion. Those affirmative pages, however, turned out to be important to the book's effect. The book had to exhibit plausible acts of criticism that were independent of the neo-Aristotelian model that it sought to invalidate. That is why the critique of John Jay Chapman's Coatesville Address, which appeared in *Rhetorical Criticism,* was consequential to the book's work of disestablishing neo-Aristotelianism. The pages on the Coatesville Address were scarcely epiphanic, but they were not an embarrassment. For the purposes of the argument, that was enough. Once anybody showed that rhetorical criticism could be written outside the governing paradigm, the gate was opened for a multitude to pass through. And they have.

Rhetorical Criticism has had a long life, as books go. It should probably be put to sleep now. The concept of literary euthanasia deserves more attention than it has received; it seems respected only in the marketing departments of publishers. *Rhetorical Criticism* is a spent force, a minor episode in the modern history of its subject. Reading a refutation of neo-Aristotelian criticism now is like reading a refutation of the Albigensian heresy. It is an antiquarian exercise.

One conviction that influenced that old book has influenced also the present one, a conviction that the intervening twenty-five years have only strengthened. It is that almost all talk about criticism is sterile. Criticism lives only in acts of criticism, not in oracular abstractions about it. Göring once said that when he heard the word "culture," he wanted to reach for his gun. I feel the same way about the prefix "meta-." The present volume is thus offered as an exploration of rhetorical criticism in the only form that its author's battered conscience will permit.

IV

Of the essays that follow, most are original to this volume and the remainder, with a single exception, have been revised for this publication. Only "Ideological Justifications" appears here unchanged, warts and all.

"Idioms of Social Identity" is an investigation of a recurrent subject of commitment, especially interesting because it so extensively affects other commitments. When social identity is an issue open to argument, the resolution of that argument is always fateful to its participants in both their public and private domains. In influencing how people talk and think of themselves and others, social identity is a rhetorically formative issue.

Because "Idioms of Social Identity" treats comparatively discourses that are identified by their common engagement with the topic of collective self-definition, the essay could be regarded as an exercise in generic criticism. Its subject and its method converge on the theme of identity, but that complementarity is mere coincidence. Neither that essay nor any other in this volume was written to conform with any methodological prescription or theoretical program. The dogmas displayed by this book are of its author's own identity. They do not solicit emulation.

"Secrecy and Disclosure as Rhetorical Forms" and "Rhetorical Secrets: Rhetorical Mysteries" are companion essays. They too are concerned with recurrent patterns in public discourse: the rhetorical manifestations of attitudes toward concealment and divulgence, withholding and disseminating, clenching the fist and showing the hand. An interest in rhetorical incompatibility—in argumentatively antipodal ideas—pervades this book, most acutely in the two studies of secrecy and disclosure.

"The Sentimental Style as Escapism" and "Authoritarian Fiction" are also companion essays, although the latter was composed more than a dozen years after the former. "The Sentimental Style as Escapism" was written retrospectively; its subject is a style that had been popular in nineteenth-century oratory and fiction, but that by the time of the essay's initial drafting in 1978 had become discredited and marginal. The more recent "Authoritarian Fiction," however, appears amidst a serious attempt to rehabilitate that style and, in consequence, to give respectability to its mind-numbing political effects. Although the sentimental style has been much studied formalistically, it has not been much studied operationally. These two essays exhibit the functional orientation that is typical of rhetorical criticism.

"Ideological Justifications" is an experiment. The manifest subject of this brief essay is an ephemeral editorial; but its latent subject is a perspective on discourse that has not been common in rhetorical criticism: the discourse as a symptom of its author. The essay seeks the ideological proclivities of an unknown rhetor, whose voice is personal but whose identity is secreted within the institutional metonymy of the *New York Times*. As an exploration of critical technique, "Ideological Justifications" is more an effort at showing than at telling—a distinction that the essay following it, "Dramatic Form in Rhetorical Transactions," attempts to clarify.

"Dramatic Form in Rhetorical Transactions" is occupied with the performative aspects of discourse. In predicating their work on the observation that performance consists of more than just words, the old-fashioned elocutionists had hold of a good idea. Their problem was that it was the only idea they had, and their single-mindedness drove their idea to the verge of an undeserved extinction. They could not, of course, have anticipated television. Its portentous enhancement of scenes and personalities has required us to rethink our assumptions about the scope of rhetorical transactions and about the centrality of argument within them.

"Dramatic Form in Rhetorical Transactions" is based on two

papers that were given at scholarly conferences in the early seventies. The creation of the essay twenty years later was, in part, prompted by the discovery that those earlier papers had been useful to some other writers. The reader who is acquainted with recent efforts to subordinate rhetorical criticism to narrative theory will recognize, in this essay, a skeptical response to those exertions.

The volume concludes, as it has begun, with an exploration more speculative than critical. "The Mutability of Rhetoric" is intended, among other things, to offer some perspective on the critical efforts that are published here. It insists on the temporality of these critiques—indeed, of all critiques—for its argument is that rhetorical forms are no more historically enduring than any other human contrivance. The essay also sponsors a vision, however obscure, of a relationship between rhetorical criticism and rhetorical theory that would give criticism a theoretical mission and theory a critical grounding.

The last chapter is, as a synoptic endeavor, a continuation of this introduction, resumed after an intervening engagement with concrete cases. That deployment is based on the scruple that generalities should be redeemed by particulars.

1
Idioms of
Social Identity

———— It takes little experience of the world to learn that not all rhetorical events are equally important. Our days are filled with importunings that are without consequence, presenting us with pedestrian selections among commodities or fashions, and we are insulated from the suasive clamor by the comfortable knowledge that neither our decisions nor our indecisions will really matter. Even a personal choice that is crucial to ourselves and to our intimates may radiate no discernably larger effect. The universe is likely to be indifferent to our private dilemmas, however wrenching, and time may ruthlessly extinguish even the memory of them. Sometimes, however, a substantial number of people confront together a choice of defining who they are, and what they come finally to believe about themselves may leave its mark on history. Such a choice possessed Americans in 1860 and again in 1965; it possessed Germans in 1932; it possesses Eastern Europeans today.

No single social identity, of course, need have an exclusive and unvarying claim on an individual. There are moments for each of us when another identity becomes salient, when, for example, some vagrant urgency may bring the ardent nationalist to be temporarily consumed by a self-conception that is entirely local or sexual or ethnic or religious or occupational; moments when the paramount commitment of a lifetime is suspended, displaced by a fugitive distraction. Each of us may occasionally coalesce with any one of a variety of groups, and there may be yet other groups to which we may never belong, but which may elicit our sympathy and support. The history of an individual passage through a multiplicity of associations is a history that can be retrieved or imagined, but its form would be biographical or novelistic.

Our focus here is not individual. It is on the aggregated participation in a composite character. It is on the single, durable social unit to whose laws a public submits and with whose fortunes they have bound their lives: that affiliation which identifies them not only to themselves, but also to others who are alien to them. Our focus is not on membership; it is on citizenship.

No collective decision is more freighted with consequence than a decision about common identity. The decision concerns no less than the predicate of further decisions, so that insofar as rhetorical function is concerned, it is supreme and controlling. And sometimes, because of how numerous the people are who collaborate in such a decision or where they are placed or when their choice engages them, what they come to believe about who they are may be consequential beyond themselves. Their resolution of themselves may be important to the world.

The current century's paroxysms of national formation and reformation correspond, in their accelerating diversity, to few other historic periods. After the Second World War, the abolition of monarchy, to which the First World War had given impetus, was brought to virtual completion. Racial subordination in the form of colonialism was everywhere challenged. And within the United States, the Supreme Court, an institution whose charge is to require the government's consistency with the nation's ideological professions, began the process of extinguishing the legal foundation of racial discrimination, mandating the reconstruction of a formerly segregated social structure. More recently, freed of censorship and repression, the voices of Eastern Europe, even among the Soviet republics, cry their claims of reflexive distinctiveness. They assert a particularistic national identity against the decaying nationalism of the Soviet Union.

The collective determination of social identity is not an everyday affair, but it is recurrent enough in human experience to tempt rhetorical interpretation. The choice of a social identity rarely occurs in tranquility. Because it is a fateful and discomfiting choice—indeed, less a choice than the assimilation of a way of choosing—the issue of self-definition is commonly manifested as an urgent crisis. The crisis is typically preceded by an agitated history: a punishing course of disillusionment with a formerly regnant social identity, a loss of faith in its efficacy and its integrity. The crisis may culminate finally in political disassociation, and the displacement of previous associations by a different configuration of social attachments, sometimes a new invention, sometimes a rehabilitated memory.

The collective renunciation of a previous identity and the adoption of a new one marks the fullest consummation of a process that can also be only partially experienced; but whether realized wholly or only partly, the process of incorporating a social identity has rhetorical characteristics that transcend the particular case. Those characteristics recur in the form of a limited number of idioms through which the issues of social identity are negotiated and, by means of argument at least, sometimes resolved. The location of the crisis does not matter, nor—within this century, at least—does its hour; its available modes of rhetorical activity remain the same.

I

Lincoln, that profound observer and masterly craftsman of American identity, concluded that the existence of slavery presented a consuming crisis of self-definition. The country could not, he thought, abide in a condition of political schizophrenia. With growing irascibility, his adversaries came finally to the same view, and the cannons spoke. But even after the unbearably sundered character of a nation half slave and half free had finally been made whole, the former slaves and their descendants retained their visibility. The epidermal distinction made it possible for old loyalties and rancors to be perpetuated in the form of a racial diremption, attended by many of the anxieties of social identity that had tormented the country before the Civil War.

A hundred years after Lee's surrender to Grant, the country was again occupied with a crisis of self-definition. Martin Luther King, Jr., led voting registrants to the county courthouse in Selma, Alabama, where they were insulted, shoved, beaten, and arrested by the minions of Governor George Wallace. In Marion, near Selma, a state trooper shot to death an unarmed man, Jimmie Lee Jackson. King summoned a fifty-mile march from Selma to the state capitol at Montgomery, to confront Wallace in his own sty. There were more clubs, more police dogs, more tear gas. Demonstrations occurred in cities throughout the country. Another march was planned, this one to last five days with a procession of fifteen hundred people. The antagonists, fixed in their colliding intractabilities, grew and collected. And the country stared at the gathering forces on its television sets, hypnotized by the spectacle of its own transfiguration. Amidst this roiling tumult, President Lyndon Johnson addressed a joint session of Congress.

Johnson's civil rights speech of 15 March 1965 is a remarkable locus of rhetorical tendencies. The speech recapitulated argumentative frictions that have scarred the history of debate on civil rights in the United States. It crystallized vocabularies of argument that are active wherever social identity is a subject of persuasion.

The speech expressed a tripartite division of attitudes, each with an accompanying idiom, concerning units of mass organization and, hence, objects of loyalty. In the historical dialectic to which that speech may be subsumed, race, section, and nation have been rivals for priority. Johnson, as the paramount spokesman for the nation, advanced the claims of nationalism to preference over race and section. Every potentially competing allegiance was assembled in Johnson's apotheosis of the occasion of his address, an occasion that he represented as the culmination of a national history embellished by the hallowed names of patriotic battles:

> I speak tonight for the dignity of man and the destiny of democracy.
>
> I urge every member of both parties, Americans of all religions and of all colors, from every section of this country, to join me in that cause.
>
> At times history and fate meet at a single time in a single place to shape a turning point in man's unending search for freedom. So it was at Lexington and Concord. So it was a century ago at Appomattox. So it was last week in Selma, Alabama.
>
> There, long-suffering men and women peacefully protested the denial of their rights as Americans. Many were brutally assaulted. One good man, a man of God, was killed.
>
> There is no cause for pride in what has happened in Selma. There is no cause for self satisfaction in the long denial of equal rights of millions of Americans. But there is cause for hope and for faith in our democracy in what is happening here tonight.
>
> For the cries of pain and the hymns and protests of oppressed people have summoned into convocation all the majesty of this great Government—the Government of the greatest Nation on earth.

Johnson proceeded systematically to establish the shared convictions of a national credo as the governing perspective from which his subject was to be viewed: "Rarely are we met with a challenge, not to our growth or abundance, our welfare or our security, but rather to the values and the purposes and the meaning of our beloved Nation."

Later in the speech, the nationalist character of the appeal was made even more evident by Johnson's recitation of the precepts that had been sanctified by blood:

> This was the first nation in the history of the world to be founded with a purpose. The great phrases of that purpose still sound in every American heart, North and South: "All men are created equal"—"government by the consent of the governed"—"give me liberty or give me death." Well, those are not just clever words, or those are not just empty theories. In their name Americans have fought and died for two centuries . . .

II

Public dialectic about race in this country since before the Civil War can be conceived as a tension among three disparate idioms: racial, sectional, and nationalistic. History, of course, is usually written by the winners, and it is therefore unsurprising that the nationalist idiom is centered in our consciousness, and that we are likely to characterize its rivals, even retrospectively, in its terms. The victory of the federal government in the Civil War and the consolidation of nationalist sentiments fifty years later through the American experience of the First World War have left Americans disposed to comprehend issues of self-definition with the perspective that Johnson's speech sponsored: adjudicating those issues by reference to a sovereign national credo.

There was nothing inevitable about the dominance of nationalism. In the American argument about social identity, the effort to establish the priority of nationalism has had two schismatic antitheses. One antithesis defined itself in terms of racial superiority and inferiority and sought to subject even nationalist sentiments to the dominion of that definition. The second antithesis subordinated allegiances both of race and of nationalism to a vocabulary of sectionalism: an ethnicity in which racial discrimination was but a single component in the larger cultural, historical, and geographical commonality that claimed the first loyalty of its adherents. Johnson's speech, which worked to reinforce the centrality of nationalism, explicitly engaged both antitheses, and one of its rhetorical merits was that it apportioned its engagement in conformity with the relative strengths of the two antitheses.

Because of his strong sectional identity, Johnson did not risk alienating sectionalists as much as a non-Southerner may have, and he was careful to cultivate that identity in the speech: "As a man whose roots go deeply into Southern soil I know how agonizing racial feelings are. I know how difficult it is to reshape the attitudes and the structure of our society."

Near the end of the speech—but, unfortunately, not near enough—Johnson drew in the most sustained way on his personal experience. His autobiographical narrative engaged both antitheses to nationalism, at once intensifying his own

regional identity and soliciting sympathy for a group suffering from bigotry. Those purposes, however, were overtaken
by a third objective that came near to ruining a splendid
speech. Johnson was concerned, and ultimately obsessed,
with providing bona fides for himself:

> My first job after college was as a teacher in Co-
> tulla, Texas, in a small Mexican-American school.
> Few of them could speak English, and I couldn't
> speak much Spanish. My students were poor and
> they often came to class without breakfast, hungry.
> They knew even in their youth the pain of preju-
> dice. They never seemed to know why people dis-
> liked them. But they knew it was so, because I saw
> it in their eyes. I often walked home late in the
> afternoon, after the classes were finished, wishing
> there was more that I could do. But all I knew was
> to teach them the little that I knew, hoping that it
> might help them against the hardships that lay
> ahead.

The portrait of the children was quick, but cogent: their
hunger, their hurt, their innocence; most poignant of all, their
eyes: the sense of baffled injury in their eyes. The auditor had
to be moved by such depiction or reject it altogether. No reserved response was possible short of disengagement because the depiction instantiated an exemplary definition of
"wrong," a categorical term. The method of the portrait had
been the method of abolitionists over a century before, the
method of William Lloyd Garrison and of Harriet Beecher
Stowe: the concrete representation of suffering, which can
leave in the mind an image that continues burning even after
its chilly and abstract contraventions have all been spent. But
at the persuasive apogee of Johnson's narrative, the speaker's
ego intruded, and the auditor, instead of being left haunted
by the agonies of children, was invited to focus instead on the
young Lyndon's good intentions. The self-referential turn in
the passage may have touched some of Johnson's former colleagues in the Congress ("Good old Lyndon"), but it deflected a powerful appeal to the country.

The egoistic detour taken in the narrative proceeded then through a miasmic swamp of self-indulgence:

> I never thought then, in 1928, that I would be standing here in 1965. It never even occurred to me in my fondest dreams that I might have the chance to help the sons and daughters of those students and to help people like them all over this country.
>
> But now I do have that chance—and I'll let you in on a secret—I mean to use it. And I hope that you will use it with me.
>
> This is the richest and most powerful country which ever occupied the globe. The might of past empires is little compared to ours. But I do not want to be the President who built empires, or sought grandeur, or extended dominion.
>
> I want to be the President who educated young children to the wonders of their world. I want to be the President who helped to feed the hungry and to prepare them to be taxpayers instead of taxeaters.
>
> I want to be the President who helped the poor to find their own way and who protected the right of every citizen to vote in every election.
>
> I want to be the President who helped to end hatred among his fellow men and who promoted love among the people of all races and all regions and all parties.
>
> I want to be the President who helped to end war among the brothers of this earth.

Lyndon the Good poses for his portrait: Uncle Cornpone with a nimbus. The passage disfigured the strongest public discourse of Johnson's presidency. It was as if some residual paragraphs from the 1964 campaign had somehow escaped being flushed from the teleprompter, and here they were, through an electronic botch, turning up in the wrong speech. Accounting for this maladroit excursus would take us into the Byzantine recesses of Lyndon Johnson's psyche, away from the more pertinent issues of social identity that the rest of his address so magisterially joined.

A strongly executed refutation of the racial antithesis to nationalism had occurred earlier in the speech when, paradoxically, Johnson's allusions were more self-effacing, and yet his signaling of his own alignments put the weight of his office more forcefully behind nationalist values:

> The real hero of this struggle is the American Negro. His actions and protests, his courage to risk safety and even to risk his life, have awakened the conscience of this Nation. His demonstrations have been designed to call attention to injustice, designed to provoke change, designed to stir reform.
>
> He has called upon us to make good the promise of America. And who among us can say that we would have made the same progress were it not for his persistent bravery, and his faith in American democracy.

Although Johnson engaged the topic of sectionalism in a sympathetic way, emphasizing his own credentials as a Southerner, his engagement with racism was less circumspect. Early and ceaselessly in the speech Johnson subsumed "American Negroes" to the category of Americans, and thereby maintained a terminological exclusion of racism from the perspective that his speech sponsored.

III

By the time of Johnson's speech in 1965, the flagrant advocates of racial identity, like Senator Theodore Bilbo or Congressman John Rankin, had disappeared from Congress. They had been replaced by more cautious and euphemistic legislators, who represented the idea of white supremacy only with a discreet detachment.

On 1 April 1965, Senator Strom Thurmond entered into the *Congressional Record,* in the form of an "Extension of Remarks," an editorial from the Orangeburg, South Carolina, *Times and Democrat* that had appeared ten days after Johnson's speech. Despite the date, Thurmond hinted at no irony. The editorial accused Johnson of inflicting on the South a revival of Reconstruction, a period when "exultant Negroes, spurred on by the carpetbaggers from the North, assumed unto themselves a blatant, braggadocio attitude." And, in turning its attention to the Selma-Montgomery march, the editorial alluded to "news reports" that the "Negroes in Alabama, led on and supported by the hundreds of Negro and white supporters who flocked down from the North, are cocky and arrogant." The words, of course, were not Thurmond's. He was only the messenger. He let others say what he may already have thought imprudent to say in his own voice.

Twelve days later, Thurmond entered onto the *Congressional Record* a radio commentary by Paul Harvey; race was scarcely mentioned, but sectional concerns were at its core:

> How long before the South will be forgiven? Only a part of the abuse which is heaped on Dixie relates to race discrimination—another large part relates to North-South discrimination.
>
> Americans, why is the race problem—North and South—but the pressure most of all on the South? [*sic*] How long before the South will be forgiven? The South lost a war 100 years ago and it is still paying for it. We forgave Germany twice in half that time.

Harvey's commentary went on to compare the generous treatment of "Germany and Japan and Spain and Mexico and everybody who ever waged war on us" with the "masochistic punishment" visited on the South, and ended, as it began, with "How long before the South will be forgiven?" Here Thurmond, again through a surrogate rhetor, had moved from a racial position to a sectional position.

Less than three months after the Paul Harvey broadcast was entered into the *Record*, the resourceful Thurmond launched a nationalist attack on the civil rights movement by blustering at the fading embers of anticommunism. In the *Congressional Record* of 1 July and 6 July, Thurmond invoked the testimony of a Yankee politician—Mayor Richard Daley of Chicago—to argue that communism had infiltrated the civil rights movement and was influencing Martin Luther King, Jr.

In a four-month period, Thurmond's trajectory had gone from the racial to the sectional to the national: a miracle of adaptation that may help to explain why, a quarter century after Johnson's proposals on voting rights had been enacted, Thurmond—near to entering the tenth decade of his life— was still a United States senator.

It is striking also to note the sources of the messages that Thurmond had delivered. The nationalist message originated with a politician—Richard Daley—with clearly non-Southern, ethnic affiliations. The sectional message originated with a broadcaster, Paul Harvey, who had no particular identification with the South. The overtly racist message, however, was given only an institutional authorship. If Thurmond knew the identity of its author, he did not disclose it. Thurmond, then, struggling against Johnson's proposals, tried every historically available perspective on race relations, but always in the voice of another and, in the case of the racist perspective, through an author who was hooded in anonymity. Although comparable enough with one another to be antithetical, the three perspectives were far from equal in their general moral authority in 1965, and Thurmond's allocation of his own association with each position mirrored Johnson's in reflecting a shrewd calculation of that position's political reputability.

The strictly and consistently sectional viewpoint was represented by Senator Harry Byrd of Virginia. On 5 April 1965, Byrd's colleague, A. Willis Robertson, entered into the *Record* a statement on Byrd's behalf. The statement was a defense of Virginia against an unfavorable opinion that the federal attorney general had expressed of its election laws. Byrd depicted Virginia as a defendant, subject to incrimination, trial, conviction, and pardon—an entity with rights and claims on justice—an organic reality. Byrd's statement was congruent with "states rights," long the political rationale for Southern sectionalism, and it was without even the hint of an overtly racial argument.

By the time of the Civil War, sectionalism had emerged

among whites as the more respectable, the more nationally influential of the two antitheses to nationalistic priority. Its spokesmen in Congress were a succession of Southern grandees, of whom Byrd was an epitome. Their idiom of social identity subordinated racial issues to the transcending exaltation of a social order that they identified as uniquely Southern. Their aristocratic gentility defined a fragile distinction between themselves and that vociferous cadre of white supremacists whose last unembarrassed representative in the Senate was probably Theodore Bilbo of Mississippi, who died in office in 1947. Bilbo's oratorical defecations had given the rankest bigotries a voice.

Less than a decade before his death, Bilbo had sponsored legislation to repatriate African-Americans to Africa. The bill received the endorsement of Marcus Garvey's magazine, *Black Man*, which urged Garvey's supporters to "give their undivided and whole-hearted support to Senator Bilbo's Bill."[1] Garvey's support of Bilbo's proposal was not the first coincidence of black and white racism. In the early twenties, Garvey had found common ground with the Ku Klux Klan and the Anglo-Saxon Clubs of America in their advocacy of racial purity and segregation.[2] More recently, Malcolm X and Stokely Carmichael have, in the Garvey tradition, demonstrated that the racial idiom in the United States is not confined to whites, just as Martin Luther King, Jr., demonstrated that nationalist appeals are not confined to presidents.[3]

Between the white versions of the three idioms and the corresponding black versions, the greatest difference pertains to the sectionalist perspective. When Southern whites defend sectionalism, it is with the presumption that within a certain prescribed territory—the South—whites and blacks will occupy segregated enclaves, and that although both groups will be subject to the same civil governance, they will be bound by social regulations that discriminate between them. The complementary African-American position cannot sensibly be called by the term "sectionalist" because it envisions no prescribed territory, such as the South, where the races are to be segregated. Rather, the races are to be dispersed, but socially segregated wherever they are, and they are to pursue distinctive economic, cultural, even religious development, irrespective of their locations.[4]

During Reconstruction, after the white claims of sectional authority had been frustrated by the Civil War, what remained were the claims of racial superiority represented by such organizations as the Ku Klux Klan. In many instances the apologetics for sectionalism were a euphemistic code for racism, both before the Civil War and after it. And it is certainly true that the subordination of dark-skinned people to light-skinned people was one of the traditional arrangements defended by Southern sectionalists, so that the two modes of argument served the same interest for many years. Yet, they are different, and one of their chief differences was the more complex conception of hierarchy associated with the sectionalist position.

The spokesmen for Southern sectionalism have often been representatives of a caucasian elite who sustain a paternalistic relationship to the "lower orders" of all races, including their own. Even the ubiquitous Thurmond, who ran for the presidency in 1948 as the candidate of the States Rights party— called "Dixiecrats" by journalists—conducted a solely regional campaign, and made no effort to excite the social resentments of non-Southern voters. Thurmond made only one speech outside the South during his campaign. Addressing the Overseas Press Club in New York City, he hewed rigorously to sectionalist doctrine:

> If you people in New York want no segregation, then abolish it and do away with your Harlem. Personally, I think it would be a mistake, but if the people of New York want no segregation, that is their right under the Constitution and no federal law would seek to force segregation upon you. And by the same reasoning, no federal law should attempt to force the South to abandon segregation where we have it and know it as best for both races.[5]

The direct political expression of white racism in America has now diminished to the strident and unheeded voices of marginal cranks. The rhetorical energies that formerly were invested in the racial idiom have increasingly dissolved into an inventory of more general populist resentments—resentments of high-born arbiters of fashion and power, of liberals who extract from others the price of their reforms, and of government itself.

As long ago as 1968, the presidential campaign of King's former nemesis, George Wallace, had become national in scope, extending even to white "ethnics" in the big cities of the North. In that election, which was the only general election in which Wallace ran for president, he was the candidate of the American Independent party. He "came close to throwing the election into the House of Representatives, getting over nine million popular votes and forty-six electoral votes." Wallace's chief difference from Nixon and Humphrey in the 1968 campaign was "in his racial myopia and his vehement criticism of the growing power of the federal government in its moves toward integration."⁶ But it is notable that Wallace did not, by then, advance a doctrine of racial identity or superiority. His animosity was directed against elites who seemed to display condescension toward the values of humble working people. Those elites were almost entirely white.

IV

The effect of a racial vocabulary is to implant within the language distinctions among racial groups. The emphasis of such an idiom is on differences rather than similarities. There is nothing intrinsically or necessarily racist about such an idiom, nothing characteristic of the idiom itself—its form or its logical requirements—that entails invidiousness. However, the idiom does sponsor race as an ontologically irreducible category, and thus creates one of the necessary conditions for racial ranking and hierarchy.

One effect of the nationalistic vocabulary is to assimilate racial differences to national values. In the case of a multiracial nation, such as the United States, the idiom provides a rhetorical vehicle for promoting amity among races through the enhancement of common ground, as Johnson's speech illustrates. Yet, no one having the slightest acquaintance with modern history can be ignorant of the destructive capacities of the language of nationalism. For the past two hundred years, the sporadic infection of nationalism by chauvinism and xenophobia has been a festering source of mass hatreds. Like a racial idiom, a nationalist idiom has its malevolent potentialities.

The sectional idiom, advanced in this country by defenders of states' rights, seems to be simply a narrower application of the nationalist idiom. Its external appeal turns on the ability of others to be sympathetic to local loyalties out of their own feelings of local loyalty. It has, however, no characteristic appeal to self-interest beyond its constrictedly defined adherents; it is inherently parochial and exclusionary. Sectionalism lacks the materials for an external appeal that argues from expediency, except for quid pro quo. When Blanche DuBois says in *A Streetcar Named Desire* that she depends on the kindness of strangers, she is being a true Southerner.[7]

The language of sectionalism before 1860 led, of course, to the Confederacy and the elaboration of a duplicate nationalism that could rival the Republic. If the effort to secede had been successful, that duplicate nationalism would have had to become the paramount idiom of the South or the area would have been balkanized, with each state sponsoring its own self-sufficient idiom of superiority in a proliferation of ever more localized nationalisms.

The relations between the dissident Soviet republics and the supervening federation of which they are parts illustrate the perspectival relativity of sectionalism itself. From the point of view of the perpetuators of Soviet hegemony, the claims of the Latvians, Lithuanians, and Estonians are narrow and provincial, but the Baltic nationalists see themselves as affirming an ultimate social configuration, one that is culturally integrated.[8] In the end, this quality of cultural integration is crucial to the dialectic of social allegiance.

The idioms of both nationalism and sectionalism can readily accommodate a racist perspective, as the Nazi movement demonstrated in its fusion of German nationalism with racism. In a similar way, Southern segregationists often proffered the idiom of sectionalism as a respectable euphemism for racism, although they frequently distinguished themselves from overt racists by sanctioning a local option and sustaining a principled tolerance for different social arrangements outside their own region, as Thurmond's New York speech illustrated.

V

Unquestionably, the most dedicated and least ambiguous representative in this century of racism as a medium of social identity was Adolf Hitler:

> The main plank in the National Socialist program is to abolish the liberalistic concept of the individual and the Marxist concept of humanity and to substitute therefor the folk community, rooted in the soil and bound together by the bond of its common blood. . . . The greatest revolution which National Socialism has brought about is that it has rent asunder the veil which hid from us the knowledge that all human failures and mistakes are due to the conditions of the time and therefore can be remedied, but that there is one error which cannot be remedied once men have made it, namely, the failure to recognize the importance of conserving the blood and the race free from intermixture and thereby the racial aspect and character which are God's gift and God's handiwork. It is not for men to discuss the question of why Providence created different races, but rather to recognize the fact that those who disregard this work of creation are punished. . . . From the chaos of disunion which had been caused by tribal, dynastic, philosophical, religious and political strife, the German nation has arisen and has unfurled the banner of a reunion which symbolically announces, not a political triumph, but the triumph of a racial principle.[9]

Hitler, proceeding from premises radically different from Johnson's and confronting different ratios of fealty, worked to subordinate the Germans' conception of nationhood to a conception of race. He was able to scant the sectional loyalties that had vexed some of his predecessors in the German chancellorship, perhaps because the common fate of the German states in the First World War had subdued sectional jealousies.[10]

It is important to note that the idioms of race, section, and nation are all reflexive in function. They all presuppose the existence of external and alien social units; each is preoccupied with its own singularity. The idiom in each case is shaped to enhance and celebrate the distinctiveness of its defining social unit; sometimes, but not always, to assert its superiority.[11]

VI

The term "kind" is illuminating to consider in connection with the reflexive functions of these idioms. Both the noun and the adjective, "kind," are derived from the Old English *cynd*, which is also the precursor of "kin." As *The Oxford Dictionary of English Etymology* notes, "Some of the words going back to [Old English] are as old as time."[12] "Kind" has cognates in a vast network of Indo-European languages and dialects, including Old Frisian, Old Saxon, Old High German, Old Norse, Gothic, Greek (*génos*), and Latin (*genus*). Variants of the term have been disseminated into the modern derivations of those tongues throughout the world.

To establish a social identity is really to determine what one's "kind" is: Who is one of us? Who is not? And to "be kind" is at once to express a gentle, generous attitude and to treat someone as one's own "kind." One's kind deserves kindness; one's kind is to be treated kindly. And obversely, to extend kindness, to treat kindly, is to deal with another being as if that creature were one's own kind.

The *Oxford English Dictionary*'s lengthy account of "kind" notes also a now obsolete sense of "Nature in general, or in the abstract, regarded as the established order or regular course of things (*rerum natura*)." We have, then, in the etymology of the term "kind," a semantic linkage among three concepts that also have a rhetorical linkage in the idioms of social identity: the concepts of social relationships, morality, and the natural order.

Even the use of the term in such a phrase as "payment in kind" reveals some of the rich moral associations with which the term has been used in its long history. "Payment in kind," which can be used straightforwardly to refer to a transaction of barter, or ironically to refer to an act of vengeance, is a phrase redolent of the reciprocity and equity that are basic to our conceptions of social morality.

The permutations of the term "kind" continue to carry with them an ancient disposition by which moral preference is given those who share one's social identity. As much as any term in the language, "kind" reflects that primeval link between social groupings and moral discriminations which marks public discourse. Preceding any judgment of value— moral, aesthetic, or even prudential—is a determination of genre. The value of a thing depends on what kind of thing it is. Determining what kind of thing it is circumscribes, in turn, what kinds of judgments are appropriate to it, what can reasonably be expected or demanded of it.

The identity of a subject is antecedent to predicating anything about it. Because the identification of a thing seems so spontaneous to us most of the time, we tend to think of such identification simply as the acknowledgment of a fact. The rock is a rock. Why do we say it? Because that's what it is. And yet, the sculptor or the stonemason may look at that same recalcitrant object and align it in their minds with a different genre of precursive experiences, seeing it as an incipient sculpture or a potential foundation stone. Our responses are shaped by such historical alignments, by acts of determining with what previously apprehended entities we should allocate a new entity, acts that decide for us the *kind* of entity it is. These determinations of inclusion and exclusion shape the distinctions and obligations, the conceptions of good and evil, even of taste and of decorum that undergird a rhetorical idiom. From convictions about what belongs with what— about kinds—course the presuppositions, the major premises of enthymemes, the common language of value that make persuasion possible.

To be sure, this linguistic evidence pertains only to the very large number of languages with terms similar to "kind," with similar etymological characteristics. However, we expect to find—and ordinarily we do find—even in an extremely exotic social unit, a special morality applicable among its members, and when that morality is extended to a stranger, it is as if that stranger had been received into the social unit. Indeed, it is doubtful that we would recognize as "social" any aggregation of creatures that did not manifest some such form of internal governance, some established code of relations that, no matter how harshly conceived, extended preferment to and imposed duties on their own kind.

To Johnson, the most important values shared by his kind were those of the founding documents. To Hitler, they were the impulses and potentialities of heredity. To Lithuanians, they are the shared characteristics of language, religion, and location. To Soviet hegemonists, they were the elements of Marxist-Leninist ideology, and more recently they have become the common fear of chaos. In each case, an audience is solicited to view its social character in terms of one prevailing and exclusionary set of perceptual values determinative of social allegiance. Each congeries of values proposes a hierarchy of identities, with one central identity dominant over inferior, sometimes competing options of identity that are placed, more or less remotely, at the margins of consideration.

In each case, with the possible exception of the beleaguered Soviet hegemonists, the audience is summoned to fulfill itself, but the cynosure of fulfillment is distinctive. Johnson, by rehearsing the moral commitments of the founding documents and summoning the nation's fidelity to that set of convictions, invoked the elective and canonical nature of the American identity. Hitler, by contrast, proposed a description of the essence of the Aryan race, and announced policies that expressed that essence. The Lithuanian appeal is to a shared body of social characteristics formed by a unique communal history—like Hitler's, a set of factual claims, historical and sociological, rather than, like Johnson's, a set of credal principles to which a public's loyalty is solicited.[13]

VII

Johnson's speech pivoted on a single sentence: "This was the first nation in the history of the world to be founded with a purpose." Whatever historical hyperbole may be imputed to the claim, its basic insight is commanding. Indeed, the United States of America is a social unit that derives its identity primarily from a set of political convictions rather than from—to mention a few of the more conspicuous possibilities—a distinctive language, or a common ethnic heritage, or a myth of genesis, or a unique relationship with divinity. That it shares with other states the condition of having a geographical location is, of course, notable, but its location serves to influence rather than to constitute its identity. America's vast internal migrations and the diversity of its local styles vitiate an exhaustive equivalence between geography and national identity. But by the account of the most famous, influential, and justly admired speech in the country's history, the nation, "conceived in liberty," was "dedicated" to a "proposition" at its very origin.

The use that Johnson's speech made of his pivotal affirmation was not historical. He spent not one moment defending the originality that he had attributed to the country's self-definition. His procedure, rather, was to adduce those statements of national value most incompatible with racial discrimination and thereby to intensify opposition to it. That procedure, and the conception of social identity that made it possible, remain instructive long after Johnson's legislative proposals have been woven into the texture of the law.

Johnson's hierarchy of value was based entirely on commitments of belief, as was that of Soviet hegemonists. By contrast, Hitler's hierarchy was founded on heredity, as perhaps is that of the Baltic nationalists. The appeal of one is to what auditors believe in common; the appeal of the other is to what auditors are in common. To be sure, the fact that both are cases of appeal subsumes both to rhetoric, but their rhetorical characters are strikingly different. The hereditarian argument is solely reflexive; insofar as it cultivates a belief, that belief is preeminently about what the believer is. The field of conviction in the alternative system is much more extensive and variegated, including, as it does, the array of values—some articulated and some inchoate—that constitute a cohesive system of principles. Issues of conviction and of identity attend both sets of experience, but in a crucially different priority and with a crucially different emphasis.

In Johnson's speech, Americans were called upon to consummate the potentialities of their shared convictions.[14] In Hitler's speeches, Germans were called upon to consummate the potentialities of their genetic character. Johnson's followers, like adherents to the evangelical tradition, were to qualify for salvation by the honest acceptance of true convictions. Hitler's followers, like adherents to the Calvinist tradition, were to qualify for salvation by having been born among the elect. While the means of persuasion were rhetorical in both cases, the groundings of argument were antithetical. Johnson derived identity from conviction; Hitler derived conviction from identity.

The violators of Johnson's code were in "willful" defiance of the Constitution and of "popular sentiment." They had, in sum, suffered definitional alienation by disdaining the two prime sources of American identity: the supreme laws of the Republic and the common convictions that undergirded them.

The violators of Hitler's code had perversely breached the natural order.[15] Indeed, his adversaries were no longer even of human form. As issue after issue of Julius Streicher's *Der Stürmer* illustrated, they were insects or rodents; carriers of infection; pests, to be exterminated.

VIII

The United States and the Soviet Union have in common that each has defined itself doctrinally. Their competition in the cold war was indeed a rivalry of ideologies. But the association of the term "ideology" with Marxist theory has obscured the fact that not all claims on allegiance, not all forms of social identity have the same relation to their adherents or the same sorts of entailments.

A social identity that is founded on a natural condition, such as heredity, affects beliefs in a radically different way from a social identity that is founded on conviction. Accordingly, there are different syntactical rules governing the representations of pedigree and conviction, manifested principally in two ways: First, a hereditarian identity is subject to criteria of factual accuracy in a way to which a convictional identity is immune. Second, a hereditarian identity is conceived of as predetermined, while a convictional identity is conceived of as voluntary.

First, concerning the facticity of the two kinds of identity: it is possible to be deficiently informed about one's pedigree, or even to be wholly mistaken about it, but one cannot be equivalently misinformed or mistaken about one's convictions. Some of our greatest dramas are hinged on ignorance of heredity. Oedipus and Jocasta are initially unaware of his ancestry and of their mutual implication in the patrimonial curse that will overtake them both. Oswald Alving, in Ibsen's *Ghosts*, does not know the origin of the blood-born affliction that destroys him. And, for comic balance, there is the delicious moment in *The Importance of Being Earnest* when Jack embraces Miss Prism as his mother. There is no corresponding syntax governing conviction.

We think and talk of heredity as a fact, as part of a natural order. In *Oedipus Rex* and in *Ghosts*, a character who suffers a tragic peripeteia is ignorant of a crucial fact that is the source of his destruction. We are brought, through the operation of the play, to see his fate as inevitable, but unmerited.

A belief, on the other hand, is not a fact of nature. It requires an act of acquisition or of commitment before it can come into existence, and it can be discarded or amended volitionally. Moreover, we hold believers responsible for their beliefs, and although a mistaken conviction can lead someone to grievous misfortune, as Arthur Koestler's novel, *Darkness at Noon* illustrates, we know that the believer can always have chosen otherwise.

One can surely have a mistaken conviction. Few of us have been so wise or so unadventurous as never to have ardently believed a silly idea. Few of us have lived such dulcet lives as never to have had our faith betrayed. We know, and we are enabled by our language unequivocally to say, that we can have a conviction that is utterly wrong. But we cannot be wrong about having a conviction. A conviction may be variable in the certitude with which it is held, the clarity with which it is understood, the duration during which it is sustained, the intensity with which it is invested; but the language does not allow one to talk of one's own conviction as variable in one's knowledge of it. To have a conviction is to know that one has it.

In Dickens's *Hard Times*, Louisa asks her dying mother if she is in pain. " 'I think there's a pain somewhere in the room,' said Mrs. Gradgrind, 'but I couldn't positively say that I have got it.' " This is delirium. In the very next sentence of the novel, the omniscient narrator refers to Mrs. Gradgrind's statement as "this strange speech." Strange indeed, for our language does not accommodate uncertainty about whether we feel or believe something. Any disassociation between the experiencing of an internal state and the knowing of it is aberrant.

When, as sometimes happens, we observe a disparity between what someone professes to believe and what that person appears really to believe, our inclination is to infer either that the person has, through some form of misrepresentation, lied, or that the person has made an error of utterance which, if corrected, would repair the disparity. Our observation would not lead us to conclude that the person is, like Mrs. Gradgrind, afflicted with a defective knowledge of her own conviction. We demand of one another the consistency of profession with action, and it follows that we attribute to one another the knowledge necessary to such consistency. To say that we are certain even of our uncertainties may risk paradox, but Descartes has powerfully argued that we cannot be doubtful about doubting. So, although we may believe doubtingly, we cannot doubt our believing.

We know whether we have convictions and we know what they are, but because we may have imperfect knowledge of our genetic origins, a condition of hereditarian social identity is characteristically attended by the possibility of mystery. We can have doubts about our origins and ancestry. Indeed, it seems a common experience for a child—even one whose social identity is not hereditarian—to wonder if it has been adopted, if its ostensible parents are its true progenitors. The prospect is opened early to the balanced mind, and permanently retained, that it may be deficiently informed. And prudence teaches each of us, sometimes harshly, that since our knowledge must be imperfect, so too must be our confidence. Hence, a hereditarian social identity carries the germ of a singular anxiety—the anxiety not of nagging doubt but of undiscovered ignorance—an ignorance of facts that, if known, may alienate one from one's kind. And so the form of reassurance necessary to the perpetuation of hereditarian identity is genealogical rather than doctrinal.

A second syntactical difference is that a social identity based on heredity is not subject to volition in the same way as a social identity based on conviction. One may decide how much value to attach to such a hereditarian identity; one may even affirm or deny the relevance of heredity in determining social identity; but one may not choose one's heredity. While the value of a heredity—a race, for example—may be a subject of persuasion, the nature of it is not likely to be. In ordinary reckoning, heredity is a brute fact, fixed and unalterable. One may, in principle at least, decide what importance to attach to pedigree, but one cannot decide on a pedigree in the way that one can decide on a conviction. A system of social identity that is based on heredity is therefore not ideological in quite the same way as a system of social identity that is based on conviction. The point at which a prospective adherent is able to exercise will differs in the two systems, as do the requirements for membership.

Whittaker Chambers's 1952 memoir, *Witness*, which captured the imaginations of American conservatives during the McCarthy era, is, among other things, an effort to show the painful consequences of ill-chosen convictions. A problem with the book is in Chambers's attempt to compensate by apocalyptical posturing for the discrepancy between his account of his youthful, witless commitment to communism, and the condition of desolated heroism that his memoir coaxes the reader to assign him. *Witness* may work as a parable, but it is unconvincing as a tragedy. A hereditarian tragedy, like Sophocles' or Ibsen's, because its causative agencies are linked to natural processes by essence rather than artifice, induces in the auditor an experience different from such attempts at "convictional" tragedy as *Darkness at Noon* or *Witness*. The true tragedy stifles at its source the small voice that whispers, in the case of Arthur Koestler's Rubashov or of Whittaker Chambers, "The damned fool got what he deserved." Our pity for another's misfortune is inhibited in the presence of complicity. Maybe it is the revenge of the timorous on the foolhardy. Whatever the reason, we do apply a stern economy of judgments to a person who suffers misfortune because of choices that others similarly situated knew to be bad.

A consequence of the differing presuppositions concerning pedigree and conviction is that a social identity that is based on conviction is the responsibility of its adherent in a way that a hereditarian identity cannot be. And that condition of responsibility, in turn, entails the logical priority of individual identity over social identity. We cannot postulate a choice without a chooser, and inasmuch as we talk of convictions as objects of decision and responsibility, then a social identity based on conviction implicitly assumes the prior existence of an individual will.[16]

A social identity grounded on conviction may at any moment be the subject of moral choice. It can be relinquished in favor of an alternative social identity. A human being who exercises choice cannot be wholly inchoate. Volition requires psychological resources and moral preferences. Therefore, no matter how politically constricting its institutions of authority, a social identity grounded on conviction integrally preserves a domain of individual choice. This ineluctable association between individualism and belief-grounded social identity lodges an incurable contradiction at the heart of efforts to grow a new kind of collectivized being from the clod of ideology, as the recent experience of the Soviet Union is demonstrating.

In the contrasting case, individualism is not entailed by hereditarian identity, although the two are not inherently incompatible. Hereditary social identity precedes individual identity. While an identity grounded in conviction can be repudiated with the assertion of a new and contrary social identity, a hereditarian identity cannot quite be replaced or denied; it can only be downgraded. The alteration of a hereditarian identity does not take the form of a renunciation: "I am not an Ibo." It rather is a transvaluation: "My being an Ibo is less important than my being a Nigerian," or even, "My being an Ibo or a Nigerian is less important than my being an African." Hereditary identity is congenital. It cannot be renounced; it can only be minimized. It attends every moment of life from the first. It is not a profession; it is a destiny.

Conviction, of course, is the object of rhetorical activity. A society whose identity is based on conviction is compelled to make provision for rhetorical activity to assure its own continuation. Such provision may not guarantee freedom of expression; it may consist only in the suppression of competing beliefs and the continuous propagandizing of people. But whatever its disposition, a social unit based on conviction must constantly see to the perpetuation of its orthodoxy; it must concern itself in a systematic way with the persuasion of its members.

A society whose identity is subcognitive—a society founded in a natural order that is independent of conviction—has no correspondingly inherent need of rhetorical activity. What are called here "hereditarian societies" are bound together by what some anthropologists have called "primordial attachments." Such an attachment is "one that stems from the 'givens'—or, more precisely, as culture is inevitably involved in such matters, the assumed 'givens'—of social existence: immediate contiguity and kin connection mainly, but beyond them the givenness that stems from being born into a particular religious community, speaking a particular language, or even a dialect of a language, and following particular social practices." [17]

The pressures and bewitchments of external influences may prompt rhetorical campaigns of revival or of purification in a hereditarian society; but left to itself, such a social identity can be carried through time solely by the conditioning influences of family, peers, and role models: agencies that a society founded on conviction might regard as private rather than public.

IX

Because social identity in America is based on conviction, American identity itself attains a provisional character that does not attend hereditarian identities. Convictions may be revised, refined, modified, adapted to circumstance. They change over time, even if that change is subtle, because the minds containing them grow older and are altered. Convictions—even dogmas—have a mutability denied the unyielding facts of heredity. Convictions form the basis of an intrinsically kinetic social definition.

By contrast, a social definition based on heredity is subject to change only through a slow accretion of subtle adaptations and accommodations. And no matter how badly pummeled by circumstance hereditarian social units may be, no matter how hostile the apostates that they discharge, they are stubborn and persistent in their conceptions of themselves. Such conceptions are not the yield of acquiescence. Their authority depends on their appearing organic, objective, and natural. Not having been acquired through persuasion, they are not dispossessed through dissuasion.

It follows that a political system founded on conviction will be more persistently absorbed in self-definition and more characteristically preoccupied with cultural formation than a political system founded on heredity. That is why the constitution of American society is being continuously written.

The writing and ratifying of *the* Constitution was constitutive in its form of action as well as in its consequence. That act of composition was not simply a codification of the means by which the aspirations of the preamble were to be realized. It was also the initiation of the continuous process of adjustment and refinement that necessarily accompanies the founding of social identity on the basis of convictions. Beliefs, to be believable, have to be attractive to believers. Convictions live only in the mind, and a living mind is inconstant. It is therefore the case that a certain intellectual restlessness is endemic to the American character. Its tensions are not entirely the products of rivalries or of checks and balances. They are also the inevitable result of a defeasible identity that must be forever renewed.

What is most fundamental differs in the two systems of social identity, one of which is hereditarian and the other of which, because it is based on convictions, I am tempted to call rhetorical. In a hereditarian system, a condition of being is fundamental, and individuals are called upon to respect the distinctiveness of their kind. In a rhetorical system, a condition of believing is fundamental, and individuals are called upon to regard their political values as authoritative.

Moreover, that claim to authority makes the inclination to proselytize a component of the rhetorical system of social identity. Moral certitudes are seldom hoarded. The impulse is to disseminate them: to make the world safe for democracy, to encourage everywhere the benefactions of the market economy, to construe self-determination in terms of popular referenda.

That is not to say, of course, that hereditarian social systems are less invasive or more disposed to laissez faire. They simply justify their intrusiveness differently. They are more reflexive, less missionary. They do not require the universal reign of virtue, and so they are not fated to be chronically irked by the world's imperfection. On the other hand, they may more greatly fear its contamination.

It should be no wonder that anti-Semitism is reported to be increasing in some of the Soviet republics as the central authority of the nation declines and, with it, a rhetorically based social identity.[18] From the viewpoint of non-Jewish nativists, the Jew is one "among us" who is not hereditarily "one of us," and wherever heredity is salient, the one who is not of "our" blood cannot share "our" allegiance. Any group assigned by hereditarian nationalists anywhere a racial or ethnic identity different from their own becomes thereby vulnerable to their social exclusion. The Russian minorities in Estonia, Georgia, Latvia, and Lithuania are, thus, objects of the same sort of antipathy as the Jewish minority is in Russia.[19]

X

The issues that we have pursued here concern the articulation of social identity: the *Gesellschaft* with which people overtly associate themselves, the ways in which they describe and warrant their ultimate social allegiance. In dealing with such complexities as social units, it goes without saying that scarcely any significant referent is autonomous. A social unit based, for example, on sectionalism as its most valued identification will, in the course of time, confirm, articulate, and exalt its distinctions of dialect, of local custom, of shared history and attitude, even of costume and diet, and all of these will become constituents of social identity, each with its own claims to perpetuation. The social allegiances with which we are concerned are precisely those that are never culturally neutral. Each of them is accompanied by a host of signs, of personal markings by which the individual is shaped to the social unit.

Any social identity shared by a group of people will tend to elaborate its own cultural characteristics, and at least some of those characteristics will stand in deputy to the social identity itself for its adherents, so that they will take a jealous pride in those characteristics and, in some cases, come to value them highly, sometimes more than life itself. It is not uncommon for individuals to take one or another cultural sign as, in fact, a cultural signature and, in an act of moral synecdoche, to invest that sign with all the value of their social identity. Thus, for example, the burning of the flag becomes a sufficient act of lèse-majesté in the minds of some Americans to warrant amending the Constitution.

Our subject here has been words: the preeminent terms by which people identify themselves: Southerner or American or Caucasian, Latvian or Soviet citizen, Egyptian or Arab. A particular exigency may, for a time, compound such terms; another exigency may disassociate them. Social identities vary widely in their mutability, but even the most adamant of them have complexity. The acquisition of a social identity, then, is not only the relatively simple matter of embracing a term or a set of terms. It is, also, the infinitely more complex act of as-

similating whole networks of affiliation, value, and vocabulary. Thus, the terms by which groups of people come to be
known, and to know themselves, have rich connotations that
may absorb the exegetical efforts of a social unit's most gifted
agents. In viewing here the idioms of social identity, we have
been concerned with the rhetorical components of those uncommon but fateful moments when elements of individual
personality blend and interact with elements of social character, those moments when fidelity to a social identity becomes
a subject of persuasion and an object of choice.

2
Secrecy and Disclosure as Rhetorical Forms

———— On a wall of Santa Maria Novella, the Dominican chapel in Florence, there is a fresco by the fourteenth-century painter, Andrea de Firenze, in which each of the seven liberal arts of the medieval tradition—the trivium and quadrivium— are represented in a conventional series of personified figures. The figure of Dame Rhetoric has her right hand open, as has the figure of Cicero, seated below her, whose palm is exposed to the viewer. Next to Rhetoric is the dour Dialectic, both hands clenched, with the figure of Zeno seated at her feet, his one visible hand, too, a fist.

The open hand, the closed fist: those icons of rhetoric and its antithesis were already ancient when Andrea rendered them. Quintilian, in the first Christian century, attributed the images to Zeno, over three hundred years before.[1] To have abided for so long in the work of such diverse artists, the symbols must have seemed not only apposite but also rich in implication. And indeed, we can still read them in a variety of ways: inclusion versus exclusion, acceptance versus rejection, enticement versus deterrence, amity versus enmity, or—what is most pertinent to the present inquiry—disclosure versus secrecy.

The emblems of the open palm and closed fist present at

least two implications for our consideration, one of which is the very incompatibility of the gestures that they propose. The oppositional tensions that ferment within a universe of discourse are signaled by its vocabulary, especially its antonyms. Public/private, liberal/conservative, radical/moderate, individual/societal: such pairs of antonyms are the matrices of rhetorical activity. They signify fields of judgment. They designate the topoi—the places—where commitments of political and moral significance are made and unmade.[2]

To refer to a rhetorical "place" is to mean, simply, that there are some locations in the field of thought where verbal controversy can occur through the instrumentalities of rhetoric, and other locations where the mode of discourse must be of some character other than rhetorical or where, as Wittgenstein has advised, one would incur an obligation to be silent.[3] The "places" where rhetorical activity may occur are marked by the presence of linguistic antonyms. They are symptoms of the capacity of language to support both an affirmation and a denial—a contradiction, either moiety of which is a linguistic possibility.

A universe of discourse in which propositions cannot be contradicted is inhospitable to rhetorical activity. The uncontradictable proposition can serve as the ground or premise of rhetorical activity, but it cannot itself be a subject of rhetorical activity. The advocacy of an uncontradictable proposition is an epideictic exercise; "mere" rhetoric; form without substance; a display, often of banality.

Because antonymity may be a locus for rhetorical activity, the thorough explication of an antonym would include an inventory of the argumentative configurations possible to it. The ways in which commitments are solicited and given—the structures of persuasion and conviction—should be illumined by such an examination.

These methodological assumptions will govern this study of the antonyms secrecy and disclosure. The thesis to be argued is that attitudes toward secrecy and disclosure are manifested not alone as articulated commitments, but also as rhetorical forms.[4] Secrecy and disclosure are instantiated as rhetorical forms in two ways. One way is in the archetypal role of translator—a role that, because of its prestige and authority, accrues suasory power to the person playing the role. The second way in which secrecy and disclosure are instantiated as rhetorical forms is as commonplaces—commonplaces with uncommon powers of implication and entailment.

II

The role of translator is ordinarily subject to a modest variety of interpretations. Some translators are experienced by their audiences as media, instruments, passive transparencies through whom a message appears to pass without distortion or modification. Other translators seem more refractive; their choices about how best to represent the original source are conspicuous in their translations. One variation among translators, then, is along the dimension of presence and it extends from self-effacement at one extreme to obvious interpretive involvement at the other.

Irrespective of how passive or active a translator may appear to be, however, the task of translation requires artfulness. It is a task that represents an achievement, a course of preparation and initiation, an apprenticeship of trial and discovery that has been expressed in ancient myths of our culture. As Tzvetan Todorov has written, "The quest of the Grail is the quest of a code. To find the Grail is to learn how to decipher the divine language."[5]

The role of translator as medium is so familiar to us that we scarcely acknowledge its existence; but the preacher, for example, who provides "readings" of a sacred text, who mediates between his audience and an ultimate mystery, is regarded as having a privileged access to arcane truths. That endowment exalts his status for those to whom he translates and confers on him an authority that extends even to the temporal realm. David Grossvogel writes of this mediator: "The intercessor becomes so much a human repetition of the concealing/revealing god that he may well be divinized in turn: the mystery swallows up its human interpreter."[6]

The translator's text is sacred because it contains the key

that will make experience coherent. Coherence, in the idiom of this ideology, is a teleological matter. To be plausible and satisfying, an account must be prophetic, because experience occurs temporally, instrumentally, purposefully; it is completed in the realization of an end. (It is no accident that the language has the word "end" signify both an objective and a culmination.) For an adherent to this form of meaning, a text that omitted prophecy would lack an essential element of the sacred; it would not awaken the piety essential to the apotheosis of the translator.

The translator can derive suasory power not only from disclosing texts. Anything at all that may have a latent meaning in addition to its manifest one is susceptible to translation and so is a potential vehicle for the enhancement of the translator's ethos. Both communism and nazism, for example, pretended to disclose the hidden pattern of history, thus transforming the followers of each movement into initiates, possessors of arcane knowledge—not simply people who believed something, but rather people who knew something.[7] Accordingly, the prophets of each movement, the master translators, were deified, even as was Osiris, the ancient pharaoh of the Egyptians, who had disclosed to his people the secrets of agriculture. In each case, the mediator of revelation became distanced into mystery. It is as if there were a formula: the more comprehensive the translation, the more recondite the translator.

The persona of the translator can as potently serve profane ends as sacred ones. We have learned of the "Manson family" that there was more behind that murderous cult than drugs and nihilism. There was also an apocalyptical ideology, and its source was in the obscure lyrics of the Beatles' songs that Manson translated for his followers into a prophetic vision: Southern California hermeneutics.[8] Here the text possessed only some of the more lurid properties of the sacred, but all the same, authority accrued to its translator. The key to meaning was the key to power.

Although the simple, even banal, lyrics of the Beatles' songs may seem an unlikely source of wisdom, Frank Kermode has observed: "Once a text is credited with high authority, it is studied intensely; once it is so studied, it acquires mystery or secrecy."[9] The sacred text, in sum, never completely yields up its secrets. The shadows may be pushed back, but they are never finally dissipated, for every revelation creates another mystery. The translator's relationship to the text, therefore, can be one of perpetual engagement.

That these last few examples—Stalin, Hitler, Manson— have been odious should not be taken to imply that the role of translator is typically malevolent. Patently, when a physician interprets a diagnosis or a philologist construes a text or a jurist elucidates a statute, well-intentioned people seeking commendable ends may have adopted the role of translator. But although this rhetorical form may be morally ambivalent, it is not politically neutral. Because the role of translator carries special status and persuasive power, it is especially suited to more hierarchical social orders. Where egalitarianism is highly valued, there the role of translator will be less likely to be played.

The paradoxical condition of those literary critics who espouse textual egalitarianism presents a particularly revealing linkage between the role of translator and the valuing of hierarchy.[10] In an effort to deconstruct—in this context, a euphemism for "discredit"—a traditional hierarchy, to repeal the literary pieties that they associate with a bourgeois tradition, these critics abjure the role of translator. They become not so much faithful servants of the text as self-assertive rivals to it. Their ideological commitment prohibits the subordination of criticism to its subject because that is hierarchical and so, in a triumph of ambition over humility, they seek to extinguish their role by aggrandizing it.

Historically, the methods and institutions of science, as distinguished from its personalities, may have come to represent an egalitarian substitute for this rhetorical form: a democratization of translation. In principle, scientific method gives everyone access to the techniques of decipherment. The historic development in which the Protestant Reformation moved to abolish priestly intercessors and to promote a conception of divine truth as available equally to all human beings prepared for and reinforced the equality of access to secular and natural truths that we associate with the scientific enterprise.

The essential antipathy of science toward secrecy and its accompanying reverence for equality of access to information is well expressed in a speech given by J. Robert Oppenheimer to the Association of Los Alamos Scientists following his resignation as director of the Los Alamos Laboratory. The speech is especially poignant in coming from one who had successfully led the members of his audience to collaborate in the deeply secretive scientific effort of developing the atomic bomb:

> There has been a lot of talk about the evil of secrecy, of concealment, of control, of security. Some of that talk has been on a rather low plane, limited really to saying that it is difficult or inconvenient to work in a world where you are not free to do what you want. I think that the talk has been justified, and that the almost unanimous resistance of scientists to the imposition of control and secrecy is a justified position, but I think that the reason for it may lie a little deeper. I think that it comes from the fact that secrecy strikes at the very root of what science is, and what it is for. It is not possible to be a scientist unless you believe that it is good to learn. It is not good to be a scientist, and it is not possible, unless you think that it is of the highest value to share your knowledge, to share it with anyone who is interested. It is not possible to be a scientist unless you believe that the knowledge of the world, and the power which this gives, is a thing which is of intrinsic value to humanity, and that you are using it to help in the spread of knowledge, and are willing to take the consequences. And, therefore, I think that this resistance which we feel and see all around us to anything which is an attempt to treat science of the future as though it were rather a dangerous thing, a thing that must be watched and managed, is resisted not because of its inconvenience—I think that we are in a position where we must be willing to take any inconvenience—but resisted because it is based on a

philosophy incompatible with that by which we live, and have learned to live in the past.[11]

Descartes's *A Discourse on Method* too was pivotal to the development of our modern attitudes toward the institution of science. Its argument, predicated on a condition of radical skepticism, purported to sweep away all received opinion, all presumption and intellectual privilege, and to confront reality with the pristine clarity of common sense—"common" here meaning "distributed throughout the human race without any difference of degree."[12]

Finally, in arguing that the institution of science has come to represent a more nearly egalitarian version of the sacerdotal activity of translation, we should note the conventions that are supposed to govern scientific publication: blind review, impersonality of style, formulary reportage, and the requirement of replicability. All of these conventions work to prevent special claims, to efface reputation, to oblige the Nobel laureate and the novice tinkerer alike to submit to the same standards on the same terms: to work as equals in the disclosure of nature's secrets.

This consideration of an archetypal role involving the divulgence of hidden meanings must be augmented by noting that there are other persuasive roles besides the role of translator, and that some of those other roles are abetted by concealment rather than disclosure. When, for example, the judge is robed, the garment neutralizes the individual appearance; it depersonalizes the wearer. The robe serves the trope of synecdoche; it proclaims the judge to be Justice. The person is concealed. Similarly, the white sheet of the Klansman obscures an angry redneck, and proposes instead an embodiment of social interests and moral emotions. It is, indeed, not the person but the role that is elevated and the subordination of the person to the costume assists this process.

III

The preacher, the prophet, the seer—each is an acolyte who serves a higher authority by transmitting a message. Each conveys precious secrets, shares hidden treasures, distributes covert values. But there is another sort of translator also meriting our attention and that is one who conducts an exposé, who seeks the disclosure of secrets in the belief that such exposure will work to the detriment of whatever is revealed—that the secret, which is simultaneously concealed because it is evil and evil because it is concealed, will shrivel in the luminosity of revelation.

Two figures illustrate such a translator—two figures who are themselves so grossly distinguishable that they constitute a moral antithesis: Sigmund Freud and Joe McCarthy. They had virtually nothing in common except the generic ground that makes it possible to contrast them. If Freud can be regarded as a Prospero of modern culture, then McCarthy would surely qualify as a Caliban. They shared, however, one attitude that is central to our present inquiry: they esteemed disclosure and mistrusted secrecy. And in sharing that attitude, they shared also—one benevolently and one malignly—an idea with peculiarly modern political ramifications.

Freud played the role of translator in deciphering the secret code of dreams. In psychoanalysis, dreams are a uniquely pure, but not the only hieroglyphic; any form of human experience may be an arcanum requiring translation. Like the totalitarian ideologies of modern Europe, psychoanalysis discloses a historical pattern: the formation and deformation of the individual psyche; the mystic origins of distortion and desire. The therapeutic technique of psychoanalysis requires the fullest possible exposure of personal secrets by the analysand to the therapist in the conviction that disclosure has purgative power, that what suppurates and corrupts in the darkness will heal in the light.[13]

Where the brave voyages of exploration conducted by Plato's Socrates probed the inherited memory of his interlocutors for recollections of an innately endowed truth, the classically trained Freud sought from his patients a memory not so much forgotten as repressed. And where, in Plato's Socrates, a dialectically induced recollection banished ignorance and assured probity, in Freud the retrieval of the repressed memory released a pent-up energy and healed a psychic wound.

Shifting the object of discovery from a mystery to a secret, and shifting also the objective of discovering from philosophical verity to emotional health were crucial to the translation of moral discourse from a judgmental and punitive idiom into a diagnostic and therapeutic idiom.

There is a certain compulsion exercised by a mystery—a requirement that the mind go in a mandated direction—an imposition of perplexity, which is an uncomfortable condition that agitates for alleviation. Mystery produces tension and it has done so at least since antiquity, when the imperative requirement that mystery be purged enkindled the play that so influenced Freud's theory, *Oedipus Rex*. The serene tolerance of a question requires a course of self-discipline, for questions demand answers and generate discontent. To answer a question, therefore, is to some degree to be freed from a lien that has been placed upon the mind. The emancipation that psychoanalysis associates with self-discovery is subjectively indistinguishable from political liberation.[14] And those who value freedom preeminently also value disclosure, while those who value order preeminently are disposed to abide mystery.

The political alignments of psychoanalysis are fully consonant with this general interpretation. Freudianism was anathema to the Nazis, and its pervasive suspicion of political ardor disables it generally as an instrument for ideologues. It is closely associated with a clinical mode of interpreting morally significant acts. Its most orthodox practitioners and adherents, convinced as they are in the persisting power of instinct over human experience, disbelieve in the perfectibility of society or in the efficacy of politics to promote human happiness.[15]

Beyond the substantive relationship between Sophocles' *Oedipus Rex* and the theory of psychoanalysis, there is a similarity of form that is important to our theme. Both the play and the theory transcribe a quest for truth, an urgently sought disclosure proceeding from a fixed and unquestioned moral base. In the case of the play, the quest is anchored in religious certitude and in the preternatural actions of the gods. In the case of psychoanalysis, the quest is anchored in a received view of health and of proper familial relationships, confirmed ultimately by the personal report of the sole and indisputable expert witness, the patient. By contrast, McCarthy represented disclosure as an instrumentality of the state, and his quest was predicated on premises that were themselves the subjects of dispute, of rhetorical activity, of claim and counterclaim. As in the story of Oedipus, McCarthy sought the purgation of the polity, but the object of his catharsis was not the violator of a divinely sanctioned taboo. It was rather a group of opponents in a temporally bounded debate.

Moreover, the catharsis of Thebes was a terminal act in that the curse was lifted and the episode concluded. The moment of psychoanalytic insight is also a terminal act in that the origins of neurosis are disclosed and its symptoms are put on a course of extinction. But the disclosure of secret agents and agencies, as McCarthy sponsored it, is not terminal; it concludes nothing beyond itself. It is ad hoc, a transient skirmish in a prolonged conflict; it functions merely to confirm the ideological position that generated it. Such a disclosure is, in sum, not purgative. It leaves the fundamental affliction in place and extirpates only one of its local manifestations. To employ one of the favorite metaphors of McCarthy's followers, it excises only single cells of the cancerous infection.

Disclosure as a mediate device, as a short-range instrument, has a character different from disclosure used to achieve ultimate, conclusive aims. And this same difference between intermediate and ultimate purposes may apply, in reverse, to secrets; that is, keeping a secret for a short-range purpose may have a character different from keeping a secret permanently. Secrecy seems always to be instrumental, probably because we do not presume in its favor, but disclosure may sometimes be an end itself. Our moral views of secrecy and disclosure are affected by that difference.

Freud and McCarthy, in radically different ways, for incomparably different reasons, and to incommensurably different effects, were both media for the transmission of a postmedieval form by which the practice of confession shifted from a secret-keeping to a secret-exposing activity.

McCarthy translated texts, associations, and ways of talking into expressions of treasonous intention. He battened on our half-conscious and barely acknowledged commitment to the curative efficacy of divulgence. McCarthy served a public that savored hidden scandals, that found conspiracy at once tantalizing and repellent, that longed for the catharsis that follows discovery and peripeteia. It is a public whose appetites have sustained generations of yellow journalists and whose prying curiosity is focused on the betrayals of overt conventionality by covert apostasy; a public nourished by the junk food of the psyche: the debauchery of the respectable, the perfidy of the reliable, and the venality of the trusted. Scandal-mongering is the rhetorical form of disclosure in an epideictic mode.

A passion for exposé is associated with paranoia and, consequently, with the paranoid style.[16] It is paranoid to believe that whatever is hidden is evil. And it is paranoid to expand beyond a modest point what one regards as symptomatic. To interpret something as a communication requires that it exhibit certain linguistic conventions that qualify it as a message. Erring in this interpretation in a chronic way by overdetermining the meanings that can be attributed to events is as truly paranoidal as the conviction that hostile conspiracies rule the world. Both are symptoms of delusion. Hence, the persistent diagnosis of all mysteries as evil or all events as morally significant is an epistemological disorder of pathological proportions. And just as the belief in malign conspiracies manifests itself as a particular style of political thought, so the exegetical deformity associated with rampant interpretation—with seeing messages everywhere in everything, with obsessive disclosure—manifests itself also as a particular style of political thought. Generically this disorder can be expected to appear mainly in forensic discourse or in those occasional deliberative discourses that claim precedent for their warrant. In the nonpolitical sphere this omnicritical impulse would appear with greatest frequency in sermons, where diagnosing it as a pathological condition would be question-begging.

In the form of paranoia associated with hostile conspiracies, the world is closed—a container of secrets—and a condition for knowing truth is to penetrate the resistant integument of appearances to gain access to what is concealed. In the form of paranoia associated with the overdetermination of messages, however, the world is animated by purpose and the sole barrier to its disclosure is the imperceptiveness of those who would spurn its testimony. As the notoriously secretive Thomas Pynchon has somewhere remarked, "The cutting edge of paranoia is the realization that all things are connected."

IV

We are accustomed to thinking of secrecy and disclosure as occurring in particular, individuated cases, but they can equally well occur over great spans of historic time. Remembering and forgetting are linked to disclosure and secrecy. They are the reflexive disclosing and secreting of past events, collectively represented in the historical myths that become enthymematic premises on which arguments may be constructed.

It is seldom that a reflexively probative history is a total fiction. There were truly heroic cowboys in the old West and there were truly villainous Indians. There were truly intrepid pilgrimages in covered wagons across the trackless desert, just as there were truly shoot-outs at high noon. These venerable elements of the mythic histories of American Caucasians were not wholly manufactured, nor were the corresponding mythic histories of the American Indians. Rather, the historic myths that intoxicate the popular imagination are composed of salient, representative characters and events distilled in a process that purifies their motives and moral qualities, and exchanges complexity for dimension and depth for definition. We fabricate our history, true enough, but not entirely of synthetic yarns. We make our collective past through selection and interpretation, a phylogenesis in which some few events are brought to great prominence and many other events are suppressed. Thus, the histories that people believe about themselves express secrecy and disclosure as rhetorical forms.

The historical exposé is a characteristic political strategy, while a deference toward the past is an equally characteristic, but distinctive, political strategy.[17] To one mode of advocacy, the historic record speaks with a thousand tongues of past malefactions that taint a present motive. To the alternative mode, the historic record stands as a model, a source of wisdom and rectitude, a condition to be retrieved and exalted. In the one case, history is a source of disenchantment; its exposure would find its immediate rhetorical end in resentment. In the other case, history is a repository of precedent; its sanctification would find its immediate rhetorical end in piety.

Unintentional distortion is a variation on the historic uses of secrecy and disclosure. In entering into that pact with the devil by which accuracy is exchanged for morale, the simple, pious villagers of Dachau knew only their own innocence, just as the simple, pious Mississippi gentry of an earlier time knew only the happy slave singing in the cotton field. In considering secrecy and disclosure thus far, we have not considered distortion as a medium of secrecy. We have equated secrecy with concealment, disguise, and suppression. Unintentional distortion is a form of disguise, but it is a disguise designed to fool oneself, to conceal something from one's own knowledge of it. Secrecy and disclosure as rhetorical forms are not employed only consciously and deliberately; but the subject of unintentional distortion brings us to the threshold of the unconscious and of the inscrutable.

A different historic possibility, though, is open to inquiry. Suppose that the diminishment of religious faith that has marked the rise of modernity increased the quantity and intensity of cosmic perplexity. Suppose, in sum, that the decline of faith generated mystery. Such a supposition would be predicated on the belief that a religious cosmology functions to explain something, that it assuages certain bewilderments and confusions, and that if it is withdrawn as a set of convictions, then those bewilderments and confusions are likely to reappear. Scientific culture does not persuasively address teleological or moral riddles. In the void of metaphysical disenchantment, the mysteries re-present themselves.

The decline of religious faith, then, could be expected to be accompanied by the increase of an oppressive dialectical entailment—a restrictive burdening of the soul—with the consequence that a condition of freedom would become a cynosure, even an object of intense longing. Certainly such an account comports with the historical record in that the ideal of political liberation is a modern, post-Christian idea, revived after a long dormancy. The account suggests another connection between the ideas of freedom and of disclosure.

V

Catholic confession involves the disclosure of secrets by the penitent to the confessor, but the confessor is in turn bound by the most solemn of oaths to keep the secrets. The point of such confession is not disclosure; rather, it is to bring the impalpable operations of consciousness under the regulation of a moral code. Thus, it represents a central tenet of the evangelical tradition that conflates the state of one's mind with the state of one's soul. The postmedieval development is to require the disclosure of secrets to the public domain. In the Catholic confession, the secret is subordinated to moral governance; in the dispensation of the Enlightenment, the secret is dissipated: it ceases to be a secret.

Of course, the very distinction between public and private spheres, between matters that are concealed and those that are open, depends on the existence of a consciousness capable of those distinctions. Such a consciousness was evidently slow to take shape in Western culture and is a comparatively recent development. Witold Rybczynski relates the character of the medieval home to the character of the medieval *mentalité*, noting that life then "was a public affair, and just as one did not have a strongly developed self-consciousness, one did not have a room of one's own."[18] He goes on to describe the origination in the seventeenth century of houses that were used exclusively as private residences, separated from workplaces, and notes that "with this privatization of the home arose a growing sense of intimacy, of identifying the house exclusively with family life."[19] Our modern sense of the self seems to have taken form only within the last three hundred years. If our present strong sense of privacy did not crystallize until after the Enlightenment, it can be no surprise that we find a functional difference between disclosure in a medieval practice, such as the confessional, and disclosure in its postmedieval form.

There is an important distinction between regulating a condition and destroying it, between being initiated into a mystery and having a mystery disclosed. An initiation into a mystery preserves the mystery. The initiate shares the mystery only with a cadre of the elect, sometimes even taking a vow to sustain their monopoly. But the concept of disclosure implies a dissipation of mystery. From an economic standpoint, one could say that an initiation into a mystery preserves the capital; an exposé expends the capital.

VI

To think of mystery economically is more than a figurative conceit. There is, in truth, a correspondence in our attitudes toward mystery and property. This relationship is manifested in the ways we commonly talk of secrets and mysteries: "Don't give away the ending." "Keep the secret." "Don't give me away." All of these phrases suggest the proprietary nature of secrecy. Our idioms themselves postulate that secrets are possessions of value, so that they can be given away as if they were benefactions.[20]

The versatility of the noun "security" is also evidence of the interconnection between secrecy and property. "Security" can refer to secret-keeping or to wealth-keeping, as well as to that diminishment of vulnerability that either condition may promote. And the verb "secure" can mean either to safeguard against penetration or to acquire. In a variety of ways, the idea of mystery and the idea of property are fused in our language.

The extraordinary popularity of mystery films in the pre-*glastnost* Soviet Union may be germane in this context.[21] Perhaps those Soviet audiences were getting some private, heretically capitalist satisfaction from those films—a materialistic equivalent to pornography.

The proprietary character of secrets has even been affirmed

in that most cautiously wrought of prose compositions, a decision of the United States Supreme Court. Speaking for the Court in *Craig v. Harney* in 1947, Mr. Justice Douglas said, "A trial is a public event. What transpires in the court room is public property."[22] The issue in the case was the power of a lower court "to suppress, edit, or censor events which transpire in proceedings before it." And it is remarkable that actions which the Supreme Court prohibited from being kept secret, the Court called "public property." The implication is irresistible that a secret that may be kept is, therefore, private property.

The association between secrecy and property is not solely a modern relationship. There were strong conjunctions among the art of miniature, the rhetoric of the sonnet, and the themes of secrecy and privacy in the Elizabethan period.[23] Those links are motivationally suggestive for our present inquiry. Both the art of miniature, with its constriction and covertness, and the Elizabethan sonnet, with its strict adherence to formal structure, propose a fiercely inhibiting activity, a quest for the control and order that, exacerbated, becomes greed in the economic realm and authoritarianism in the political. The fusion of these impulses—retentiveness, secretiveness, and a desire for dominion—illuminates the psychological dynamism behind the proprietary character of secrets.

In addition to the proprietary character of secrets, we should also note the secretive character of property. We can appreciate it best if we think not of our own possessions, but of another person's. Our property, of course, is available to us and familiar, but another person's property is likely to be concealed from us: in a box, in a drawer, in a safe. Records of it are stored in a ledger or a bankbook and kept private, confidential. Even when we have a special access to another person's property—as a houseguest, or by having found a lost article, or by dealing with the effects (note that word) of a sick or a dead person—those personal possessions have an alien, enigmatic aura. We are conscious of their having a history of which we are ignorant. Property is a private matter, intentionally mysterious.

Like other private matters, proprietary possessions are not

uniform in their character of mystery. Our conception of owned objects arranges them in varying proximities to ourselves, so that we apprehend our nearest possessions as projections of ourselves (eyeglasses, for example, or personal jewelry); then the next more proximate as personal items (clothing, for example); then beyond those are possessions held in common by groups of varying intimacy from families to polities (kitchen tables or city parks); and finally the possessions of strangers, which vary yet further in proximity depending on the remoteness of their owners. Beyond all of these objects, possessed or subject to possession, would be objects that we apprehend as unpossessable and therefore in a separate domain (rivers, mountains, cultural monuments). Associated with each of these gradients of proprietary interest is a corresponding gradient of mystery, with the deepest mystery associated with the unpossessable.

The vow of poverty taken in a religious order has its implications for the renunciation of secular mystery: I shall secrete no possessions and possess no secrets. Possessions create mysteries, and a renunciation of possessions therefore expresses an aspiration toward complete candor. Reservations, qualifications, doubts—these are all properties that our language makes us capable of having, of retaining, of keeping secret. To refuse to own anything is to own up to everything. The vow of poverty exposes the will. The ascetic induces a revelation by becoming one.

There is a barter implicit in the vow of poverty: In return for eschewing private and personal mystery, the ascetic hopes to gain the treasure of an ultimate disclosure. He is now possessed, but by a supernal agent. His talk of himself and his condition becomes, by conventional standards, paradoxical and arcane. He has acquired a different reflexive idiom because he has become mystifying in a different way—mystifying no longer because, like most of us, his inner life is guarded and obscure, but rather because it has ceased being guarded and obscure. He must therefore discuss himself in ways that are cryptic to us because we are not accustomed to hearing them. The ordinary language, which conflates mystery and property, may not be appropriately applied to him.

Reflexive exposure has created relational mystery. He must be accounted for in necessarily abstruse ways, so that the very idiom demanded by his new condition is a source of mystification.

The old aphorism that we are known by our possessions has some truth to it. Our things acquire significance not only to ourselves but also to others' apprehension of us. But there is also some sense in the proposition that we are unknown by our possessions—that our properties obscure us and we them.

In *The German Ideology,* Marx and Engels argued that mystification is necessary to achieve the disparities of property typical of a capitalist economy.[24] Maybe so, but the relationships between mystery and property go well beyond simply providing a screen for proprietary inequalities. Our ways of talking about mystery and property are extensively interchangeable and closely related. Mystery is not merely an instrumental requisite to property, but an essential part of its nature.

VII

Attitudes toward secrecy and disclosure are not autonomous. A preference for either the exposure of secrets or for their preservation is embedded in a congeries of other attitudes, and is a fallible sign of those other attitudes. The inclination to keep secrets signifies a general parsimony; the valuing of privacy accompanies the valuing of property. Conversely, the wish to expose, to make public, to disclose, is highly compatible with a wish to disburse, to distribute, to make possession equal and uniform.

This systemic character of beliefs about secrecy and disclosure raises the possibility that fictional works that are importantly concerned with secrecy and disclosure—detective stories, for example, or any works that we might designate as mysteries—could affect different audiences in different ways, depending on the audience's prior attitudes toward secrecy and disclosure. For example, the prime source of satisfaction for one reader of a detective novel may be in its being mysterious until the end, while the prime source of satisfaction for another reader of that same novel may be in its solving the mystery at the end. One reader would gain more satisfaction from the concealment and the other from the disclosure.

More demonstrably, there are fictional mysteries that work to obviate one of those sources of satisfaction and promote the other, so that they are, in their effect, partisan mysteries. A genre of popular entertainments, illustrated by the Frankenstein movies or "The Incredible Hulk" television series, has as its theme the unhappy consequences that flow from delving into too many secrets. Such dramas are interpretable as rightist moral tales. Another genre that exalts the unravelers of mystery is illustrated by some movies that were made in the forties, including the canonizing biographies of Louis Pasteur and of Marie Curie, as well as the Sherlock Holmes and Charlie Chan series. Those entertainments are interpretable as leftist moral tales. In one case—the monster films— demystification is the evil. In the other case—the detective films—mystification is the evil. The one pivots on the condemnation of an action—the breach of nature's secrets. The other pivots on the condemnation of a condition—the unknown. The genre of fiction that condemns an action is affiliated with the general political opinion that actions produce conditions. The genre of fiction that condemns a condition is affiliated with the general political opinion that conditions produce actions.

Vincent Canby, reviewing some mystery films, wrote: "Whodunits are politically conservative, being artifacts of a well-ordered world where all questions have answers, all debts are paid and all crises rise and fall with tidal predictability."[25] Canby's specific judgment can be disputed, but his ascription of a political character to mysteries is striking and wholly plausible.

Siegfried Kracauer was equally occupied with the politics of mystery:

> In 1913, the detective film emerged [in Germany]. . . . It is noteworthy that, while the French

and Americans succeeded in creating a national counterpart of Conan Doyle's archetype, the Germans always conceived of the great detective as an English character. This may be explained by the dependence of the classic detective upon liberal democracy. . . . Since the Germans had never developed a democratic regime, they were not in a position to engender a native version of Sherlock Holmes.[26]

Goebbels, who presided over the Nazi film industry, had what David Stewart Hull called "an aversion to crime films."[27] Perhaps it was simply a personal aversion, but if it was, it was an exceedingly convenient one, for it comported with his politics. The inquiring mind of the detective, the undistractible pursuit of truth, the dedication to disclosure, the veneration of impersonal laws—these are certainly not compatible with nazism. But a certain genre of mystery is: "Goebbels had a somewhat lunatic, if well-justified, obsession with the activities of fifth columnists, and pounded the message of spies on the homefront."[28] Accordingly, the Nazi Ministry of Propaganda sponsored films whose villains were sinister agents of foreign powers and whose heroes were those who protected secrets.

The activity of espionage has a relevance to the theme of secrecy and disclosure that extends well beyond Germany and the Nazi era. After more than three decades, a fitful controversy continues over the case of Julius and Ethel Rosenberg—the American couple who were executed in 1953 for having spied for the Soviet Union. In many ways the Rosenbergs personified issues that attend the politics of secrecy and disclosure. Their alleged disclosure of secrets—indeed, of the ultimate secret of state, which is the means of universal destruction—is well adapted to the general aggrandizement of disclosure that characterizes the Left. And concomitantly, their disclosure of the ultimate secret to the ultimate enemy constituted for the Right the ultimate evil, for which the ultimate penalty was appropriate. In the Rosenbergs, then, we had an amalgam of the supreme mystifier (the spy), the supreme informer (the thief of atomic secrets), and the supreme victim (they were Jewish). It is no wonder that this case continues to gnaw on our imaginations.

Spies, espionage, and the culture of secrecy have acquired an intricate form in their popular conception. There is an expectation that the spy is not bound by the ordinary rules of morality. Having ruptured that vital scruple associated with openness and sincerity, the expectation is that other constraints, such as an inhibition about killing or stealing or betraying, would also become violable. The spy is a Nietzschean character whose existence is in a moral realm incommensurable with our own, answerable to principles and actuated by sentiments that are alien and mysterious.

The duality of the spy's condition—the radical disparity between his public face and his private character—and the calculated secrecy that is required to maintain that disparity compound to generate a consuming state of consciousness. The loyalties that constitute prima facie expectations—obligations of the normal moral order—are set aside by the spy, subordinated to his professional interest, perhaps even exploited, so that his secret life represents a true transvaluation of values.

We make an important distinction between a private life and a secret life. A private life is simply one shared only with intimates, conducted without attracting notice. Everyone is expected to have a private life. But a secret life is one attended by potential scandal, one in which there is discrepancy between appearance and reality, between reputation and character. To say that someone has a private life is to utter a banality, but to say that someone has a secret life is to imply something sinister. A private life can be boring, but a secret life never is. The secret life is concealed even from one's familiars, but a private life is lived among them.

Tempting as it may be to believe that the difference between a private life and a secret life is one of degree, our common discourse renders them quite distinctive. We do not talk of privacy and secrecy in ways that suggest continuity between them. We therefore should not equate public/private with open/secret.

There is a difference between having a secret and having a

secret life. A secret life is a habitually suppressed mode of conduct; its revelation is invariably revelatory of character. That is seldom the case with a secret.

VIII

While the tensions between secrecy and disclosure as rhetorical forms have been at the center of this exploration, there are other, related terms that also reflect some of the same oppositional and ideological characteristics. The multiple meanings of "open," for example, illuminate some of the contradistinctions between secrecy and disclosure. A hand may be open, a secret may be open, a door or window or curtain may be open, a person may be open, a countenance may be open, a store may be open or opening, a show may be opening. The opposite of open is closed. A hand may be closed into a fist, a door or window or curtain may be closed, a store may be closed or closing, a show may be closing; but a secret cannot be closed and it is not really clear that a person or a countenance can be.

The relationship between "closed" and "close" is raised by the question of whether the "close" relations among members of a "closed" society are any more than a terminological coincidence. "Close" relates to distance, proximity. "Closed" relates to access. Containers and apertures can be open or closed. Being open or closed always involves some object that has a potentiality for being known or concealed. The container of or window onto that object is open or closed. A mere empty space, whether surrounded by a material surface or as an interruption in a plane, could not be open or closed unless it could contain something, literally or figuratively. There are also lexical variants on the verb "close" that entail ideas of putting together, aggregating, negotiating, whose political implications are apparent; and of terminating, concluding, and dying, whose implications, if any, are not apparent. And although a phonological account of "clothes" would probably argue for its being an accidental pun on the verb "close," the semantic correspondences are remarkable, for we are enclosed in clothes that hide our hides, concealing our privates from the public.[29]

"Closet" too is relevant: a place where objects are contained, sometimes concealed. "Close" and "closet" have the same etymological roots; both are related to ideas of secretiveness and of secreting something away as well as of enclosures and containers that impress their contents.

In governmental circles, secret information is "classified" and information to which the public is allowed access is "unclassified." It is easy enough to understand how these terms came to be used in these ways: In conformity with the law, a formal action must be taken to designate something an official secret and thus to make its disclosure a crime. Such an action is a "classifying" in the strictest sense. Yet, we must observe the general associations of the term "classified" with ideas of having been contained, enclosed, encompassed within a category, placed in a class, ranked. We have but to extend those associations to the political sphere to see again a remarkable consonance between the idea of secrecy and the ideas of hierarchy and order.[30] Correspondingly, something that is "unclassified" can be generally interpreted to be undefined, indefinite, uncontained, without fixed identity: free.

Finally, the Florentine representation of Dame Rhetoric reminds us to note "close-fisted" in contrast to "open-handed" in terms of niggardliness in contrast to generosity. That distinction is especially striking in light of the relationship between secrecy and property. It would strain credulity to suppose that these intricate associations, embedded in the language, do not reflect and influence attitudes.

IX

The magnification of openness and candor is strongly related to the promotion of sincerity as a virtue. Behind the reprehension of secrecy and hypocrisy is an abhorrence of any disparity between appearance and reality. It is necessary to this orientation for one to be able to read the manifest surface of things as an undistorting facet of their real character. The most exhaustive expression of this orientation is pantheism, which holds that ultimate reality, both metaphysical and moral, pervades all phenomena indiscriminately, and that the humblest object may therefore be examined for the profoundest disclosures. Where, moreover, incoherence and spontaneity are cultivated as social desiderata, the existence of a supremely coherent mind behind the social diversity can be the source of a reassuring faith.

To prize sincerity is to demand that things be what they seem. The opposite of that demand is not so much the denigration of sincerity as it is a resignation to the impenetrability of surfaces, an acceptance of the insolubility of mystery, an adjustment to permanent bafflement. One orientation resists secrecy and the other accepts it as inevitable.

A set of highly artificial social mores, of elaborate practices of makeup, costume, masks, social role inversion, and ceremonious behavior, is the playful counterpart of a tolerance of secrecy. This epideictic expression flirts with the possibility of elevating insincerity to the status of a virtue. The royal court of eighteenth-century France, with its rococo minuet of decorum, is an example of a place where this game was played out. Perhaps the game finds its champion player in nineteenth-century Britain in the persona of Oscar Wilde, who sponsored the priority of art over nature, who cultivated an ostentatious artifice in appearance and language, who expressed contempt for the moral inflation of sincerity and sentimentality, and who lived an elaborate secret life. Wilde's example is all the more conspicuous against the background of his Victorian milieu, which sought to internalize artifice in the form of sentimentality so that even its hypocrisy could be transmuted into sincerity.

Theater is an institutionalization of this playing with secrecy. The theater is a place where otherwise unacceptable incongruities between appearance and reality can be enacted. A moral drama of pretense, a celebration of the opacity of masks, is always the play in the theater, irrespective of the play advertised on the marquee.

The institution of the theater denies the transparency of

surfaces; it affirms the essential hypocrisy of things. The theater is constitutionally incapable of representing the virtue of sincerity. It lies even as it proclaims itself as true because it is an institution dedicated to fabrication. The theater is bound to be mistrustful of appearances, to project them as unreliable and evanescent. It can explore an extremely wide range of metaphysical possibilities, ranging from solipsism through naturalism to supernaturalism; but the coincidence of surfaces and realities cannot be convincingly advocated through the medium of theater. It cannot finally redeem appearance. Theater cannot even be a venue in which secrecy is persuasively discredited unless the theatrical devices of discredit have their own secrecy preserved. The theater is a secret-keeping institution. Its efficacy depends on its discretion.

The very word "hypocrite" is derived from the Greek term for actor. Yet, the closest that the theater may come to sincerity is in the emotions that an actor can feel in embodying a character. The Stanislavskian tradition especially has made much of regarding the actor's incorporation of genuine feelings as a form of risk-taking, and the risk is precisely that of self-disclosure.[31] One does not go to the theater to see people be themselves. Indeed, there is even a sense in which one does not go to the theater to be oneself. As a member of the audience, one is instead a special, social being with a special, social set of sensibilities and constraints, a person in the temporary role of suspending disbelief, an actor in the role of spectator.

The theater presents a paradox: While its nature is to dissemble and proffer deceptive appearances as putative realities, its most historically visible dramatic form has been that of consecutive disclosure. The first act asks a question that is finally answered in the last. And so the paradox is that an institution bound to artifice is formed to yield disclosure. Drama puts fakery at the service of truth.

There are certain modes of disclosure that are adapted to certain genres of secrets. For example, the confessional is a mode of disclosure adapted to the secrecy of motives. Pornography is adapted to the secrecy of sex. Science is adapted to the mysteries of nature. Translation is adapted to the secrecy of codes. Theater is adapted to the secrecy of agents; it is the place where dissembling is public.

X

Although we seem to have generic relationships of complementarity between secrecy and disclosure, there is a curious lack of symmetry between them on an ideological level. Our regnant attitudes toward secrecy and disclosure are not entirely coherent. We may have a general distaste for secrecy, but it does not follow that we are uniformly comfortable with disclosure. A substantial number of us would endorse the proposition that concealment is bad—always and everywhere, bad—and that ideas or acts, institutions or policies or persons that are open, honest, natural, or spontaneous are praiseworthy. By contrast, a probably greater number of us would endorse the proposition not that concealment is good, but—in a variant on Pope's overused line—that knowledge can be dangerous. This commonplace has been rehearsed in a popular series of cautionary tales from the fall of Adam and Eve to the latest variant on *Frankenstein*. The moral is always the same: One can inquire too far. One can reveal too much. Some things are better left unknown. Some mysteries should be left alone.[32]

We can, then find people who are unqualified in approving of openness, but we can find no one who would be unqualified in approving of secrecy. The range of attitudes that our civic culture makes available to us does not include an unconditional approval of secrecy, corresponding to the unconditional approval of disclosure. We need not seek far for the reason: If someone undertook to live in conformity with an unqualified approval of secrecy, that person's life could take no form other than an extremely hermetic misanthropy. And that, in turn, suggests the source of the asymmetry: We can conceive of a social order instantiating total disclosure. Probably some families and tribes approach this condition. But we cannot conceive of a social order instantiating total secrecy; such a condition would constitute not a social order at all, but rather a Hobbesian chaos of nasty and brutish solitude.

The ideological contrast between secrecy and disclosure, then, is no less than the contrast between individualism and communitarianism, between heterogeneity and homogeneity. An idea of a heterogeneous society entails respect for secrecy, for privacy, for individuality and personal freedom, for the cultivation of distinctiveness and of a clear differentiation between the public and private realms. An idea of a homogeneous society entails respect for disclosure, for openness, for common goods and civic virtues, for generous public access to personal matters.

This contrast requires two qualifications: One is that secrecy can be associated with individualism only to the extent that secrecy is not the exclusive practice of an elite coterie. A society dedicated to a homogeneous ideal will still conceal secrets in its ministry of defense. It will not, however, advertise privacy as a social ideal.

The other qualification is that aspirations toward individualism and communitarianism are ordinarily mixed and often in conflict within each of us. And even where these separate impulses have been resolved, their resolution has more frequently involved a compartmentalization of experience than a synthesis of the impulses. Some archetypes will serve as examples: The member of the John Birch Society is a material individualist but a spiritual communitarian. He favors the individual disposition of objects in the form of property and goods, but he favors communitarian structures for the regulation of feelings. The flower child, by contrast, is a spiritual individualist but a material communitarian. He favors the individual disposition of feelings in a freedom to choose narcoses or sexual partners, but he favors communitarian structures for the regulation of objects in the form of property and goods. Each seems to abide with a tension that is anathema to the other, but the implicit conviction in a reciprocal link between secrecy and property—shared in common by the Bircher and the flower child, even as they share a common language—makes the ideology of each subjectively coherent. Each may be confusing, but neither is confused.

We are able finally to identify two distinct publics, each clustered about its own defining commonplaces concerning secrecy and disclosure. One public, convinced that concealment is bad, is disposed to embrace an associative plexus of values and to accede to arguments that are warranted by those values. The values include disclosure, openness, sharing, being equal, being unacquisitive. And the other public, convinced that some knowledge can be dangerous, is disposed with equal commitment toward a plexus of values that includes privacy, private property, hierarchy, capital accumulation, individuality. These groups differ in their politics, in their sexual attitudes, in their views of science and of art, probably even in what they eat and drink and wear on their backs. But those differences are unstable and some of them are superficial. At a deeper, less mutable level, these publics are distinct from one another in the rhetorical forms to which they respond.

Rhetorical forms are elements in that system of assent that defines a public consciousness. The rhetorical forms of secrecy and disclosure are especially definitive: They reflect the ways in which people assimilate themselves to those two sovereign antonyms, the public and the private.

3
Rhetorical Secrets:
Rhetorical Mysteries

————— Let us begin the account with World War II. During that war, the public was advised that "loose lips sink ships," and that a judicious secrecy was a civic obligation. The prevailing conception of secrecy was that of concealment from a shared, external enemy, and there was a virtually universal consensus about the identity of that enemy and about the rectitude of opposing that enemy. The war made it obligatory to guard public secrets.

What does it mean to talk of a public secret? Secrets would seem by definition to be private. A public secret is one that is known only by fiduciary agents; it is concealed from all except those agents on behalf of a collectivity whose members, although not privy to the secret, have an interest in its concealment. A private secret, by contrast, is one that is concealed by the decision of someone with a personal interest in the concealment. Our focus here is on public secrets, and it was those secrets that we thought should be kept during the Second World War.

Two years after the end of the war, the public opinion polls began recording a massive shift in American attitudes toward the Soviet Union and the threat of communism. The Soviet Union, which had been our ally against the Axis powers, became our adversary, and we acquired a conception of the enemy as internal as well as external. The regnant metaphoric representation of our national antagonist shifted from the octopus of nazism to the cancer of communism, and this replacement of the octopus metaphor by the cancer metaphor was a very significant symptom of a convictional transformation. It was a shift in the conception of the enemy from an exoteric adversary who attacks, envelops, and suffocates to an esoteric corruption that is covert, debilitating, and inexorable. Concealment was now a practice of one portion of the social organism (organized, significantly, into "cells") against the rest of the organism. Secrecy, then, ceased being a civic obligation and became in the public mind an instrument for the betrayal of society.

I

Richard Nixon's Checkers speech, with its elaborate pretense of candor and its effort to amalgamate a public issue with private, personal matters, represents a peculiarly challenging episode in the unfolding of the secrecy/disclosure diremption. Indeed, the speech was pivotal in helping to shape attitudes toward the realms of the public and private, especially as they bore on Nixon's political career. Much of the Checkers speech can be explicated in terms of the secrecy/disclosure antonymity, and it can then be set in a context that emphasizes Nixon's influential role in the structuring of the antonymity during the postwar period.

Nixon, the discloser of Alger Hiss's secret identity, rose in politics as a representative of the growing reaction against secrecy. Hence, his having harbored a "secret fund," as it was extensively called in the press, was especially discrediting.

The story of the fund broke on 18 September 1952 with a front-page headline in the *New York Post:* "Secret Nixon Fund!" On the second page, the story of the fund was published under the headline "Secret Rich Men's Trust Fund Keeps Nixon In Style Beyond His Salary." These headlines were distortedly unconnected to the newspaper's account of the fund. The news report itself made no mention of the fund's "secrecy." But it was the motif of the headlines, not of the news report, that was taken up by newspapers throughout the world, and the themes of greed, influence, and bribery were subordinated to the theme of secrecy. It may well have been Nixon's vulnerability to that theme that made the distortion irresistible to journalists.

This publicity was lethally dangerous to Nixon's career, first because self-interested secrecy was antithetical to public sentiment, and second because Nixon—a prime mover of that public sentiment—was made to seem inconsistent and hypocritical by being secretive. He therefore had to conquer the issue of the secret fund or perish politically, and there is every evidence in the speech that he understood his own situation in roughly that way. Equally, it was the way that Eisenhower understood Nixon's situation.

"I don't want to be in the position of condemning an innocent man," said Eisenhower to Nixon on the telephone on 21 September 1952, two days before the Checkers speech. "I think you ought to go on a nationwide television program and tell them everything there is to tell, everything you can remember since the day you entered public life. Tell them about any money you have ever received."[1] Disclosure, then, was the antidote, the sole and urgently prescribed corrective to the political toxicity of secrecy.

The moral elevation of disclosure had been celebrated in a series of congressional hearings designed to "expose the Communist conspiracy." No exposé had been better publicized or more definitively vindicated than Nixon's of Hiss. The Associated press quoted Nixon as saying during the Hiss investigation: "The hearing is by far the most important the Committee on Un-American Activities has conducted because of the nature of the evidence and the importance of the people involved. It will prove to the American people once and for all that where you have a Communist you have an espionage agent."[2]

True to his word, Nixon's pursuit of Hiss, resulting ultimately in Hiss's imprisonment for perjury, helped to fashion an indissoluble link between an evil secrecy and the machinations of Communists. The Hiss case was the most notorious example of such a link, but not the only one. The testimony of witnesses before the House Committee on Un-American Activities had been reiterating the connection well before the appearances of Whittaker Chambers and Alger Hiss. Indeed, Nixon himself, six months before, had been rehearsing the motif. On 10 February 1948 the witness before the committee on Un-American Activities was Arthur Garfield Hays, the prominent attorney, representing the American Civil Liberties Union. Nixon said: "I think, Mr. Hays, that you apparently did not get the impression that both Mr. Hébert and Mr. McDowell [members of the committee] tried to make, and that is that the majority sentiment on this Committee is against definitely outlawing the Communist Party as a party. At the present time the majority sentiment of the Committee is toward exposure more than suppression."[3]

The association of communism with secrecy continued to be hammered by witnesses even after Hiss had gone to prison and Nixon to the Senate. A parade of former Communists, in the course of publicly confessing their shameful pasts, referred to the secrecy of Communist activities as a major source of their disenchantment.[4] Even among those—and they were numerous—for whom the House Committee on Un-American Activities was an unconvincing instrument of exposure, the connection between malign secrecy and communism became a matter of firm conviction. Eric Bentley, whose study of the committee was far from sympathetic, wrote as a troubled liberal:

> It is characteristic of liberal writing of the time (1950) that so little is said of Communism. The whole problem is seen as that of the witch-hunters themselves. On one point, however, McWilliams [Carey McWilliams, author of *Witch Hunt*] shows more curiosity than did the liberalism of the day: secrecy. Generally this was passed over almost as if the CPUSA was as open in its dealings as any other group. . . . the difference from Communist practice is not one of principle but of degree; but moral differences are often differences of degree; such differences can be enormous. The Abolitionists

had a deserved reputation for integrity. The opposite is true of the Communist parties of the Stalin era.

Descending from the high plateau of politics to simple personal prudence, one might defend American Communists who were secretive to avoid losing their jobs. Surely secrecy of that sort is often fully justified. If only the secrecy of the CP had stopped there! But not only was it a Machia-vellian scheme of life with widely spread nets, it was a veritable mystique, respected and adhered to beyond all rational plan. It was a way of life. And therein more than a revolution was betrayed. Marxism was betrayed. The whole tradition of rad-icalism was betrayed.[5]

Because, following the Second World War, secrecy had been revalued as a characteristic weapon of the enemy, and because it had come to be conceived as practiced by one seg-ment of society against the rest, and because our virtuous se-crets—most notably, the secrets of the atomic bomb—were not even exposed by this secretive enemy, but rather were surreptitiously stolen and then concealed within the impene-trable walls of the Kremlin, thus malevolently compounding the secrecy of secrets, the moral quality of secrecy was impor-tantly qualified. It was still good to keep secrets from the enemy, but it became even more intensely evil for some of us (now, traitors) to keep secrets from the rest of us.

More recently, the animus of Colonel Oliver North's testi-mony before the committee investigating the Iran-Contra af-fair was to disassociate members of Congress from "us," and make them into conduits to the enemy, thus warranting North's concealment from them of his activities. North's con-ception of his own situation was an echo of the fifties, and it found resonance precisely among those who, for one reason or another, retained the prevailing political obsessions of the fifties. One could have surmised at the time of "Ollie-mania" what has since become abundantly clear: that the anachronis-tic perspective that North sponsored defined the limits of his appeal, and assured that his popularity would be insular and transitory. Since there is no virtue in being au courant, there is no judgment implied in the observation that Oliver North and his public exhibited a perspective on the world that had reached its maximum popularity thirty-five years before, and had been in decline since.

From the postwar period to the late sixties, there was an approved class of secret-keepers. They were those who acted in a fiduciary capacity, who kept secrets from the enemy on our behalf. Then came Vietnam, and Lyndon Johnson, and the Tet Offensive and the growing, painful realization that the official keepers of our secrets had corrupted the governing values of secrecy/disclosure by illicitly keeping secrets from us. They had used the system to lie. The response was a suspicion of official secrets, a reaction in which the secrets that were kept on our behalf came to be regarded as morally equivalent to the secrets wickedly kept by our enemy. And Nixon paid the price in the Watergate scandal.

In the early stages of the Vietnam War, the popular fictions of the mass media displayed an approving fascination with secret agents and secret agencies. There still remained a class of secrets—"our" secrets—that were neither sinister nor ominous. These values were celebrated in such popular entertainments as "The Man from Uncle," "Secret Agent," "Get Smart," the James Bond novels and films, and the early John le Carré novels. During our calamitous engagement with Vietnam, however, the political ratio of secrecy and disclosure shifted again, and secrecy lost influence to disclosure as a popular intoxication. This change in the power of rhetorical forms culminated in the scandalous disclosures of the Watergate episode.

Watergate represented a paroxysm of disclosure—a reaction against the previous fascination with secrecy. Sordid as the Watergate scandal was, there may have been some truth in the claim made by some of Nixon's defenders that Nixon had been no more errant than his predecessors, especially his two immediate ones. Rather, he simply had the misfortune of living into a time when a supervening cycle of disclosure, together with its attendant righteousness, overtook him.

Richard Nixon himself sensed not merely a connection between Vietnam and Watergate, but a connection that had something to do with secrecy. In his *Memoirs,* referring to a crucial press conference on 15 March 1973, he wrote:

> It was during this conference that for the first time I began to realize the dimensions of the problem we were facing with the media and with Congress regarding Watergate: *Vietnam had found its successor.* [*sic*]
>
> I also knew immediately—even while I was answering the questions in the way that Dean and I had discussed and agreed upon—that our current approach to Watergate was not going to work. We were already on the defensive. We were already behind. We already looked as if we had something to hide.[5]

We live still within the apportionment of values created by that reaction to Vietnam, and it is manifested most markedly in the altered conventions governing journalistic discretion. The private lives of politicians are legitimate grist for journalists; and personal scandals that in the sixties would have been rigorously confined to the private arena have become in the nineties socially sanctified objects of "the people's right to know."

In the *Edinburgh Review* of September 1831, Macaulay published "Boswell's Life of Johnson," a review of a new edition of the work. The ribald and spontaneous Boswell has virtually nothing in common with the rigid and uptight Nixon, but Macaulay's comments on Boswell have relevance here:

> There is scarcely any man who would not rather accuse himself of great crimes and of dark and tempestuous passions than proclaim all his little vanities and wild fancies. It would be easier to find a person who would avow actions like those of Caesar Borgia or Danton than one who would publish a daydream like those of Alnaschar and Malvolio. Those weaknesses which most men keep covered up in the most secret places of the mind, not to be disclosed to the eye of friendship or of love, were precisely the weaknesses which Boswell paraded before all the world. He was perfectly

frank, because the weakness of his understanding
and the tumult of his spirits prevented him from
knowing when he made himself ridiculous. His
book resembles nothing so much as the conversa-
tion of the inmates of the Palace of Truth.[7]

Macaulay's commentary on Boswell conceives of a disorder
that manifests itself in excessive disclosure, a disorder in
which turpitude is aggravated by proudful boasting of it. Macaulay regards the social and characterological weaknesses
that he imputes to Boswell as aggravated by Boswell's cheer-
ful candor.

The commentary is suggestive for Nixon in its implicit allusion to a certain system of decorum regulating self-
disclosure, a system that was acutely dear to Nixon's Silent
Majority, but a system that Nixon only imperfectly mastered.
Where Macaulay's Boswell was exuberantly and heedlessly
disclosive—actuated by "the weakness of his understanding
and the tumult of his spirits"—Nixon was tensely and inadvertently disclosive—actuated by the imprecision of his calculation and the inhibition of his spirits.

Nixon's political enemies would readily have proclaimed
that his discretion was flawed. They despised what they regarded as his crude sanctimony and the unction with which
he lathered his scheming. But unlike Macaulay in his judgment of Boswell, Nixon's enemies were not especially attentive to his discretion, at least not consciously so. Their concentration was on matters that they regarded as more
important: Nixon's adversaries were preoccupied with the
corrupt values that they believed his discretion worked to obscure.

Nixon's core of followers, however, while certainly not indifferent to the probity of public figures, were acutely sensitive to discretion, to appearances, to maintaining the integrity
of surfaces. The Silent Majority was governed by sentimental
values that worked to restrict perception to the aesthetically
admissable. Their taste was for an aesthetic of order, of symmetry, of control. Not for them the spontaneous efflores-
cence, the dissonances of the aleatory, the shock of incogni-
tion. Theirs was an aesthetic of denial, a purgative and

escapist aesthetic that sought purity through the joint regulation of their perceptions and the objects of their perception.
To them, the repression of what they regarded as ugly was at
least as important as the cultivation of what they regarded as
beautiful. And when the subtle fault in Nixon's self-
censorship widened to a fissure in Watergate, his most approving followers were the ones most bitterly shocked.

Nixon suffered an additional liability in Watergate, and that
had to do with the extraordinarily dramatic structuring to
which the Watergate episode was susceptible. Unlike moral
perplexities or metaphysical mysteries whose resolutions re-
treat into infinity as each answer raises additional questions,
the Watergate mystery could be answered with finality by the
successful pursuit of a simple question: Was Nixon culpable?
Senator Howard Baker put the mystery in the form of two
famous questions: What did the president know? and When
did he know it? But these were really instrumental inquiries
designed to resolve the question of culpability. And so the
dramatic form of successive disclosure, leading finally to the
ultimate disclosure, entranced the country. It achieved an im-
placable momentum that made it impossible for Nixon to
evade the disclosive pattern.

Moreover, not only did the Watergate episode display an
architectonic structure of disclosure, its very building blocks
were disclosive in character. They consisted of the testimony
of witnesses—most, reluctant—and the piecemeal revelation
of the contents of the tapes, each revelation the product of
legal struggle. The case against Nixon was constructed by the
arduous extraction of one item of evidence after another, with
Nixon caught inexorably in the role of protecting secrets, of
seeking to frustrate disclosure, of aligning himself with the
side of a polarity that he had spent his career discrediting.

Oddly enough, the Hiss case, which initially established
Nixon's reputation on a national scale, was equally a dramatic
mystery that was capable of final resolution, so that Nixon
was associated in the public mind with the very form that
overtook him in Watergate. The playing out of the Hiss case
was, however, less dramatic than Watergate because at a crucial point in the unfolding of the drama, the scene shifted to a

courtroom, interrupting the pattern, and the national audience had to receive the denouement through the mediation of the press. Those mediators were competing for attention with the partisan mediators of the Left and Right, and the magnetism of the affair became less potent at the point at which the actors disappeared from the stage of legislative hearings. Watergate, by contrast, represented the perfected enactment of form that had been deflected in the Hiss case. The virtual universality of television as a medium, the willingness of the Senate Watergate committee and of the House Judiciary Committee to have their meetings televised, and the miraculous existence of the tapes that contained the ultimate answer, all combined to make the drama overpowering. Nixon, once the ineluctable investigator, now became the foredoomed suspect. And because he had always asserted his public and private selves with an awkward incoherence, there were those among us whose compassion was not stirred by the torturing irony of his disgrace, who, in fact, savored it with illiberal pleasure.

At a later date, Edward Kennedy's scandal at Chappaquiddick posed a mystery whose elements of titillation should have equaled those of Watergate, but the public was not equally amused. The reasons for the disparity in interest are many, but one may well have been that Nixon was closely associated with a pattern of inquiry and disclosure, while Kennedy was not. The manner of Nixon's undoing was dramatically forceful, echoing, as it did, precursive undoings that Nixon himself had contrived, most notably, the undoing of Hiss.

Kennedy's squalid mystery had, by comparison, an imagistic autonomy. Although some of the circumstances attending the tragedy at Chappaquiddick comported with rumors about Kennedy's private life, it echoed nothing in his professional career. It was interesting in the way that scandals are interesting, but it did not present a form of successive disclosures that could sustain interest over time, nor did it recapitulate a pattern with which Kennedy was associated in the public mind. It seems also likely that a successful suppression of evidence frustrated the development of dramatic momentum in the Kennedy case. Shrouded by a conspiracy of silence, Kennedy could not be pursued, and so, unlike Nixon, he was able to elude the desperate metamorphosis from a wounded animal into a prey.

II

We have been considering secrecy and disclosure as rhetorical forms that may vary over time, forms whose temporal variations can drastically alter the relationships between rhetors and their publics. There is another aspect of the subject that equally well solicits our attention. It is the character of mystery in rhetorical relations.

One could distinguish among speakers according to the extent to which they are reserved or disclosive, the extent to which they leave the impression of having withheld or bared themselves. Some rhetors create mystery by producing ambiguities—signals and suggestions that solicit interpretation, but that cannot be interpreted simply or easily. Other rhetors appear, in their discourses, to reveal everything that wants revealing, including exactly the responses that they expect from their auditors.

Daniel Webster, for example, would be a rhetor who sponsored little ambiguity, and whose disclosive character would approach the absolute. His public discourse was so designed that it raised virtually no questions about his private life or internal experience. It was discourse that answered all the questions that it raised. Webster's discourses leave no questions hanging in the air—no questions about Webster, about what he believed at the moment of his utterance, about what he wanted his audience to believe. Webster's public addresses were predicated on an audience of utter passivity, an audience that needed to invent virtually nothing, to think virtually nothing, to compose virtually none of its own responses. He wanted, demanded—indeed, created—an inert audience, a tabula rasa, a being of complete plasticity that might be moved, might be warmed, might be agitated, but that was never riddled by ambiguity. Whatever Webster's message—whether delivered in a courtroom, on the floor of the Senate, or in the open air—it was a message that left its audience as it had found them. They were importuned by Webster, sometimes, to add a belief to their inventory of beliefs, but they were never required by him to reconstruct themselves or even to compose within themselves some contestable rendition of his meaning. They had simply to repose in a condition of admiring receptivity to his eloquence.

Lincoln, by contrast, was a figure who opened a variety of interpretations. He demanded responses that he did not fully define. Lincoln continuously projected the existence of private reserves withheld because his discourses characteristically conveyed a moral complexity that exceeded their ostensible subject. Or, to put the same matter in a different light: Lincoln's discourses typically ruptured the constraints of ordinary context. He spoke and wrote with overtones that could not be exhausted by his public situation; yet, what he disclosed was coherent and compatible with what seemed hidden. He generated mystery, and he brought his audiences to baffle themselves in its resolution.

Lincoln elicited complex responses from his auditors, but he did not reveal himself to a degree proportional to those responses. No one could have. The archetypal memories alone that he evoked—the suffering Christ, the raw frontiersman, the village wit, the subtle lawyer, the rural innocent— were by themselves so complex that more than a century's exegesis has not exhausted them. Hence, the relationship that he established with his auditors generated mystery. There is always an inexhaustible quality to Lincoln's prose— even his most casual prose—a quality that suggests to us a mind behind the discourse that is never more than partially contained within the discourse.

Fanatics—the Lyndon LaRouches of the world—unambiguously demand a response without eliciting one, so that they are at once definitive and negligible. If an auditor is the least unwilling to respond in exactly the way the fanatic demands, the auditor is disengaged. There is no latitude for the auditor to participate in the creation of the response. It is like buying an article of clothing that cannot be altered: if it does not fit as it is, then it must be spurned. The message of the fanatic is unadjustable. For an auditor who is weary of thought, this very imperviousness can be an attraction. But the message of the fanatic will find acceptance only in the minds of those who, for whatever reason, require the total exogenous structuring of their convictions. Thus, it must have been the case that Hitler found, in Germany, an audience that already craved a dictator. The only question to be resolved was the form that the dictatorship would take.

It is not alone the sentimental overdetermination of a Webster or the fanatical clarity of a Lyndon LaRouche that demystifies the relationship between rhetor and audience. A less dramatic but still apt example would be Calvin Coolidge. He was verbally parsimonious. He was reserved. He was not self-revelatory; yet one does not associate mystery with him. He elicited a response that did not exceed his disclosures. The very equivalent proportioning between what he retained/disbursed and what he demanded yielded an austerity of effect in which no ambiguities were generated. Coolidge entered into a relationship with his auditors that was barren of enigma because of the sheer economy and conventionality of his claims on their beliefs.

Ronald Reagan is an interesting figure to integrate into this theory. He had no well-defined role in relation to secrecy and disclosure. His private life was not known to exist insofar as the public was concerned. And indeed, if the testimony of his son and daughter is to be believed, his detachment from ordinary familial relations suggests an exceptionally attenuated private life.[8]

Reagan forcefully conveyed the message that he was neither more nor less than what he appeared to be. There seemed about him no disparity between appearance and reality of the sort that can haunt most of us. Interestingly, his critics accused him of being totally submerged in a praxis of appearance; his supporters, of course, thought him well-connected with reality. The gravamen against him, however, was not that he was inconsistent or hypocritical. Even his detractors conceded—and deplored—the singleness of his ostensible character.

One of the considerable rhetorical benefits of his condition is that the issue of sincerity was not raised by Reagan's public performances. Rather, his persona displayed a seamless quality, so that the public man was not obtrusively artificial. His outbursts of anger ("I paid for this microphone!"), his gallantry during his injury from bullet wounds, his tearful speech at Normandy—these sorts of public events circumvented the distinction between public and private by implying someone whose public persona was not a special contrivance designed to safeguard the secrecy of a private life. If there is any price to be paid for such coherence, it is privately exacted in the poverty and formality of intimate relations—a payment that is obscured and without public cost.

The typical explanation of Reagan's ability to project a coherent persona originated in his experience as an actor: The presidency was a role, and the old trouper played it. I think it more probable in Reagan's case that a talent for fusing the public and private areas—ultimately perhaps, a kind of simplicity, a streak of the saintly idiocy glorified in Russian novels—accounted for his success both as an actor and as a politician. This is not to suggest that he was either saintly or idiotic, in the ordinary senses; but rather, that his was an ethos undefiled by complexity, freed of intrusive diffidence, uninhibited by any scruples too elaborate for economical expression. His public persona projected an unriddled mind, serene within its own limits but conscious of their existence; a mind clear, firm, and comfortable in its convictions; a mind whose self-knowledge was precisely calibrated to display neither irresolution nor affectation. It was a mind integral to the abiding poise that marked his public demeanor, a poise that functioned as a symptom of the unity of his public and private selves.

Provided a role not be attended by intricate motives, Reagan demonstrated throughout his career in film and in politics that he could assimilate such a role thoroughly and play it convincingly. His public discourse, like Coolidge's, was not a source of mystery, but it compensated him by projecting an easily comprehensible, bidimensional persona, integrated, candid, unconcealing. The greatest threat to that projection came with the Iran-Contra scandal, and that threat was precisely that the public, upon believing that Reagan had sanctioned North's Byzantine machinations, would suspect Reagan of being less simple than they had thought him to be. Reagan's self-invention required the rigorous coincidence of his public and private aspects. The shadow of mystery would have darkened his reputation.

III

A discourse that is weighted heavily on the side of disclosure becomes private rather than public in character, apologetical or confessional, dismissable, ignorable. Such discourses do not engage the auditor at the level of inference in the same way that argumentative discourses do. Instead of advancing a proposition that would constitute the minor premise of an enthymeme, the major premise of which would be supplied by the auditor, the confessional discourse advances a proposition that solicits from the auditor a moral judgment of the proposition—a moral judgment that the auditor is free to withhold or to transform. Hence, such discourses have a more precarious relationship with their auditors; they are less engaging than argument. To be indifferent to argument is to forego an ordinarily obligatory participation in a cultural-linguistic activity. But to be indifferent to a claim on one's moral attention is a natural, easy, frequent event. Every time we ignore the testimonial endorsement ("I lost eight pounds in one week"), we are demonstrating our freedom to disengage from excessive disclosure. The entire genre of apologia may be susceptible to this analysis.

At the opposite end of the scale, a discourse that lacks reflexivity, that is weighted heavily on the side of eliciting response, can appear manipulative, artificial, contrived, "rhetorical." It advances unearned convictions. Too facile a discourse, one that projects ostentatious efforts to manipulate response, is unscarred by that internal struggle for truth that is supposed to mark the earnest person. Such a discourse is, for that reason, wanting in the virtue of sincerity, and so it strikes a contemporary audience as morally deficient. The Talmudic tradition in Judaism and the evangelical tradition in

Christianity both sanction a struggle for truth, and require that convictions be the product of study and reflection, even suffering. Although the origins and forms of truth are disparate in these two traditions, they do sponsor in common a respect for the internal quest. And the secular application of that value yields the moral economy of sincerity and hypocrisy.

The evidence that an internal struggle has occurred is not the sole symptom of sincerity. There are other ways in which sincerity is manifested, and other situations in which such manifestations are expected. But the display of an earned conviction declares to the audience that the rhetor has an inaccessible inner life and a body of experience that is singular, alien, and concealed. Thus, an obfuscation—a mystery—is created in their relationship.

When Edmund Muskie wept in public during the New Hampshire primary because his wife had been impugned by a newspaper, his ambition for the presidency was ruined. He had lost self-control. And when Michael Dukakis responded coldly to a hypothetical question about the rape and murder of his wife, his candidacy was damaged. He had an excess of self-control. His inhibition made him seem mechanically inhuman.

Public personae are governed by implicit standards of self-control, standards against which one may be measured as either deficient or excessive. One way of characterizing Nixon would be to observe that he was constantly reminding his audiences of those standards, constantly claiming credit for his adherence to them, and thus constantly making the issue of control salient. He controlled his decisions—and boasted of it in his various memoirs. He sought to control events, he controlled his language and vocabulary, he controlled his emotions (most of the time). His self-control was tested in situations that were utterly out of control—the mob scene in Venezuela during his South American tour as vice president or the occasions when Eisenhower was ill with coronary, stroke, and ileitis. Nixon stayed calm and self-possessed through all of these episodes. There are also, of course, notable instances of loss of self-control: the press conference following his defeat for the governorship of California ("You won't have Nixon to kick around anymore"), or his pushing his press secretary, Ron Ziegler, during the tense period of Watergate, or his shattered farewell to the White House staff.

Nixon made control salient, not only when he lost it, but more important, when he exercised it. The effect of Nixon's repeated reminders that he refused the temptations of ease, of vindication, or of political advantage was to rehearse his audience in the implicit claim that he was inhibited by scruples, that he exercised control. And what is control, in this context, if it is not the conscious withholding and dispersing of information about tortured motives, the exercise of censorship, the regulation of disclosure? Spontaneity in a rhetor strongly suggests candor, and its opposite—manifest self-control—is associated with guardedness, with secrecy.

To leave in the mind of an observer the impression that one exercises unusual control can have obvious rhetorical advantages. The observer will gain confidence in one's steadiness and in the rationality of one's decisions. But it can also have disadvantages, and the principal one is that it raises the possibility of deceptiveness. The sincerity of a self-controlled person can become a subject of skepticism, a matter not so much of suspecting hypocrisy as of lacking confidence in sincerity. And a consequence of this disquiet is the creation of mystery in the relationship between the observer and the observed. Thus, manifest self-control can provide the important ingredient of mystery in a political relationship. It can provide reassurance of immunity to panic or hysteria, but it also introduces an element of distrust, a reservation of wholehearted commitment. It is a symptom of private thoughts, of concealed attitudes.

The most eloquent discourses are those that somehow balance withholding and disbursing to the point that they beget mystery. Enough is disclosed to license the authenticity of the rhetor, but that same disclosure signals its own fractionality, leaving the audience aware that what it has come to know is not all there is to be known.

The remaining question—itself a mystery—is why a mysterious component should be necessary or desirable in the convictional relationship. What inferences can possibly be drawn from the existence of a mystery, by itself? One inference, of course, is that the distanced persona has an inner life, and is not simply a medium alone, a neutral transmitter of messages. In antiquity, when the role of oracle was institutionalized, there must have been an immediate utility in the ability to distinguish between one whose convictions had been earned and, hence, who was responsible for them, and one who was only a passive conduit. We should note that in the *Phaedrus* and the *Symposium*, Socrates becomes such a conduit at crucial moments in the dialogue, and we are given to believe that at such moments, we have left the realm of dialectic and of argumentative procedure, and that we are receiving a uniquely pure message, unsullied by the distortions of human perception. So, one signal given by the existence of rhetorical mystery is that the message is within the realm of argument.

The realm of argument itself is bounded by two mysterious domains. One is a desert of barren expressivity that fails to lay sufficient claim on the auditors' attention to engage their inferential participation. The other is a venue of transcendence that does not engage the auditors' inferential participation because it is conclusive and complete, and requires no logical or discursive supplementation. The realm of argument, then, is bordered by vapidity on one side and revelation on the other. It is only within the realm of argument that auditors may be actively engaged. Confronted with vapidity, auditors lack the motive to be engaged; confronted with revelation, auditors lack the competence to be engaged. The one induces a passivity of indifference; the other, a passivity of deference.

4

The Sentimental Style
as Escapism

———— In a section of *A Grammar of Motives* called "The Temporizing of Essence," Kenneth Burke noted the tendency of some writers to express essences in terms of origins and vice versa.[1] Burke attributed this "double vocabulary" to the pun in the word "priority," which can be used either in a temporal or logical sense.

There are a couple of other terms that, even more clearly than "priority," are at the semantic nexus of the origin-essence interchangeability, and they are worth noting. The words are "form" and "genre."

The word "form," used nominally, refers to the shape, the structure, the essence of a thing. And used verbally, as in "to form," the sense of the word is to constitute, to shape or mold, or to originate a thing. We find a corresponding distinction between the nominal "genre" and verbal "to generate," the noun referring to essence and the verb to origin.

Adjectivally, our common usage observes a distinction between "formal," which refers to essence, and "formative," which refers to origin, although the roots of the two adjectives are obviously in the word "form." The same distinction applies to the adjectives "generic" and "generative," with their roots in "genre."

To a striking extent, then, the terms "form" and "genre" are functional mirrors of one another. They exhibit the same nominal, verbal, and adjectival variants. They possess corresponding bipartite usages. They parse concomitantly.

Clearly the two words are not synonyms. They signify differently. But even in their lexical distinctiveness, the terms "form" and "genre" still bear a remarkable relationship to one another, and that relationship is one of dialectical complementarity.

In Platonic dialectic, an inquiry about the nature of a Form led, when it was successful, to a definition composed of a Collection and a Division.[2] The terms "genre" and "form" have the same relationship to one another as do the Collection and Division of Platonic dialectic. That is, the genre of a thing is its class—a statement of its relations to all other commensurable things. The form of that thing is its inherent structure—a statement of its constituents and their relationships to one another. Genre refers to the place of the thing in the universe and to its generation as an adaptive and relational entity. Form refers to the constitution and individuality of the thing and to its formation as an entity sufficiently autonomous to be identifiable. Taken together, the words "genre" and "form" are complementary in that "genre" refers to external relations and "form" refers to internal relations.

In Platonic dialectic, the Collection and the Division together constituted the most exhaustive attainable description of whatever reality was their subject. There is simply nothing excluded from the categories of analysis and synthesis. So too it would seem that genre and form together constitute exhaustive topics for the description of whatever artifact is their subject. And considering the remarkable complementarity of the terms "form" and "genre," it is reasonable to suppose that the elucidation of either aspect of an artifact would stand to elucidate the other. That is, any information one may acquire about the form of an artifact may be heuristic for its genre, and vice versa.

This last consideration—the heuristic reciprocity of form and genre—is one that can be tested only in criticism. And since I believe that it is only by doing criticism that we can illuminate criticism, I turn now to the subject of the sentimental style, and continue my inquiry into form and genre through the medium of a critical paradigm.

To study the sentimental style, we must move backward in time to the century before our own. Whether the sentimental style is now an archaism or has survived in some form into our day is a question to be reserved for later. But there is no question that in the nineteenth century, at least, in America and in England, at least, there flourished something that can properly be called the sentimental style, and if we want to be sure of observing that style in situ, it is to that century we must turn.

II

During the nineteenth century in America, the Oneida Community was surpassed only by Brook Farm in its celebrity as an experiment in communal living, and in at least one technique, the Oneida Community was preeminent. The Oneidist guru, John Humphrey Noyes, believed in free love and the exaltation of sexuality, but he realized that the community required some method of birth control that would comport with its unorthodox sexual and social doctrines. Noyes preached and the Oneidists practiced as best they could a method of withholding sperm during copulation simply by the couple's not moving. And the technique by which the couple did not move was to think very, very hard of something spiritual.[3]

The image of a man and a woman, coupled, motionless, racking their minds with supernal fantasies, is a potential subject for ribaldry, but nonetheless the image will serve nicely as a master trope for the nineteenth century. The sort of strainedly bifurcated mentality that was carried in the Oneida Community to what surely must be its ultimate development is exhibited in varying degrees throughout the nineteenth century—the inclination, when pressed from all sides of the consciousness by an insistent demand whose presence one wants not to acknowledge, to think very, very hard of something spiritual.

Such frantic indifference—the calm in the eye of an emotional storm—did not begin with the nineteenth century any more than it ended with it, but that century displays so assiduous and pervasive a cultivation of this willed distraction that the characteristic becomes a key to the time. The public life of the century both here and in England was marked by this characteristic, and it is my thesis that the sentimental style—so admired in the nineteenth century—was not only an apposite expression of willed distraction, but also an ingenious instrument for its realization.

I should not proceed further without some effort at definition, and I can think of no better way of clarifying the sentimental style than by example. The example I submit is from an epideictic address by Daniel Webster, and it is Webster's epideictic that can serve as the paradigm for the sentimental style. Attend, if you please, this passage from the Bunker Hill Monument Address of 1825. Webster is commemorating the fiftieth anniversary of the Battle of Bunker Hill, and he turns to address the aged veterans of the Revolution who are seated in a section near the speaker:

> But the scene amidst which we stand does not permit us to confine our thoughts or our sympathies to those fearless spirits who hazarded or lost their lives on this consecrated spot. We have the happiness to rejoice here in the presence of a most worthy representation of the survivors of the whole Revolutionary army.
>
> Veterans! you are the remnant of many a well-fought field. You bring with you marks of honor from Trenton and Monmouth, from Yorktown, Camden, Bennington, and Saratoga. Veterans of half a century! when in your youthful days you put everything at hazard in your country's cause, good as that cause was, and sanguine as youth is, still your fondest hopes did not stretch onward to an hour like this! At a period to which you could not reasonably have expected to arrive, at a moment of national prosperity such as you could never have foreseen, you are now met here to enjoy the fellowship of old soldiers, and to receive the overflowings of a universal gratitude.

But your agitated countenances and your heaving breasts inform me that even this is not an unmixed joy. I perceive that a tumult of contending feelings rushes upon you. The images of the dead, as well as the persons of the living, present themselves to you. The scene overwhelms you, and I turn from it. May the Father of all mercies smile upon your declining years, and bless them! And when you shall here have exchanged your embraces, when you shall once more have pressed the hands which have been so often extended to give succor in adversity, or grasped in the exultation of victory, then look abroad upon this lovely land which your young valor defended, and mark the happiness with which it is filled; yea, look abroad upon the whole earth, and see what a name you have contributed to give to your country, and what a praise you have added to freedom, and then rejoice in the sympathy and gratitude which beam upon your last days from the improved condition of mankind![4]

Such examples of the sentimental style could be multiplied from discourses of the time.[5] Webster's effusion is an acutely sonorous representative of the type, delivered by one who knew how to keep his metaphors unmixed, how to quote copiously from Latin poetry, and how to find his way through labyrinthine periods without disappearing into the cul-de-sac of a subordinate clause.

The most notable feature of this style is the detail with which it seeks to shape response. No scintilla of reaction is left for the auditor's own creation; every nuance of effect is regulated by the speech. In the passage quoted, there is not a degree of heat or a single drop of moisture that is left to the option of the auditor. The sentimental style seeks a total control over consciousness; that is its principal defining characteristic.

The sentimental style is notable not so much for its stately movement or its piling on of figures or its tendency to tear passions to tatters, although all of those properties are often present. Rather, the *function* of those properties defines the style. Their function is didactic. It is to instruct the auditor in responding, to regulate every shade of the auditor's feelings as the speech unfolds.

Webster in the Bunker Hill address shuttles back and forth between images that could be painted on the ceiling of a chapel and descriptions of internal states and emotional seizures. The speech interlocks the two bodies of referents—the depictions and the sensations—to the end of commanding the audience's responses. They were to experience certain feelings in the presence of certain images. Behind Webster's procedure was the possible assumption that without appropriate instructions, the audience might not know what to feel, or they might feel improperly—that their spontaneous reactions could not be trusted.

In a milieu in which emotional expression is severely regulated, as it certainly was among genteel folk of Webster's time and place, a special caution will be exercised in those circumstances in which strongly emotional expression is allowed. The sentimental style is a superb instrument for such a situation. It not only elicits affective experiences, it also defines and delimits them. It enables the emotions to be given a re-creation under sanctioned auspices.

Lincoln's epideictic efforts later in the century provide an instructive contrast to Webster's. Lincoln was disposed to place more reliance than Webster on the uninstructed propensities of his audiences. Lincoln, understanding better than Webster the puissant symbols of popular religion, confidently cast political propositions in that idiom and trusted that the audience would generate for itself a religious reverence for national principles.

One of the reasons that Webster's style now seems archaic to us while we can continue to admire Lincoln's is that Lincoln's discourses are less overtly manipulative. Lincoln provokes and constrains our responses, but he compels us to make them ourselves. Webster is more intrusive and detailed. He wants to control not simply the response but the exact manner of its expression, and in this piling on of regulatory minutiae, Webster finally leaves us with nothing at all to do except to be completely malleable. Leaving no latitude to the auditor, demanding strict attention to the speech for every nuance of the engagement with the speech, Webster requires of his auditor so exacting an allegiance that the auditor can, in the end, have no consciousness of Webster's persuasion except as persuasion. The method of the communication becomes the communication, and its substance is pushed to the periphery. Thus, the auditor is disposed by Webster's very rhetorical techniques to view his speeches as display. And if—as would be the case with someone reading Webster's speeches now—an auditor were at all inclined not to grant the absolute surrender that the speeches demand, that auditor would be likely to note a discrepancy between the speeches' implicit claims about themselves and their actual effects. That discrepancy would produce the very disengagement that the speeches strive so ostentatiously to eradicate.

A quality of Lincoln's that is missing from Webster is ambiguity, but it is ambiguity of a special kind. Lincoln has no special ambiguity in the propositions and proofs of his discourse; their meanings are neither remarkably vague nor remarkably multiple. Rather, the ambiguity attends the auditor's experience of the discourse, which is left unstructured. Lincoln gives the auditor the boundaries of experience, but requires the auditor's own invention of it.

In creating room for the auditor's active participation in the rhetorical transaction, Lincoln left it open for later generations—such as ours—to play their own variations on his themes. But Webster, leaving nothing to be created by the auditor, restricted his audience to those whose emotions would work and be expressed exactly as he required. Thus, the subtlest change in sensibility stood to make Webster's speeches obsolete.

Webster was a pedant. His speeches were not only preening celebrations of his vast learning and his capacious memory and his linguistic facility; they also were compulsively and excessively didactic, in the manner of the pedant. He overinstructed. Permitting no chance response, he prohibited spontaneity. He required those auditors who would honor the claims that he made upon them to surrender themselves totally to his speeches. That very requirement works to distance auditors, to focus them on the disparity between what the speeches imply about them and what they actually are. The auditors are thereby made into spectators, connoisseurs, observers of rhetorical performances. And the rhetorical performances themselves become display.

The oratory of display is such functionally. A discourse functions as display when, intentionally or not, it promotes an incongruity between its actual audience and its implied audience. If we, as its actual audience, sense this incongruity, we begin to view the discourse as a collection of technical virtuosities. We are overhearing it, eavesdropping. We may, for various reasons, be sympathetic to the discourse and hope for the success of the rhetorical transaction, but the difference between that condition and the condition of being the auditor to the speech is the difference between passivity and involvement.

The question remains, why were Webster's epideictic efforts so popular with his contemporaries? Even granting that we today stand outside the speeches, it still is the case that the nineteenth-century public admired them. Why? Why did the public of that time so admire discourses that left them with so little freedom to form their own responses?

One is tempted to account for this popularity in terms of emergent conventions of response—to attribute it to the very inchoateness of the system of responses that by the end of that century was to be much more definite to people. But the temptation must be resisted because, in fact, there were already old traditions of rhetorical response in this country, reaching back into the seventeenth century, responses at which Americans, according to Tocqueville's testimony, seemed indeed notably adept.[6] The reason, I think, is rather to be found in the evasiveness of this style. It was popular because it provided the audience with unambiguous cues which, in their very definiteness, excluded alternatives, and thus induced the audience to be unconscious of incipient stimuli that might have uncomfortably solicited their attention. This didactic quality, then, and especially its popularity, should be taken as a symptom of disquiet and unease, of a subtly gnawing conscience and a tacit agreement to repress.

Perhaps in the case of Webster and his audience, it was the

presence of slavery that had to be repressed. For what are still not fully understood reasons, the West was not able to assimilate the institution of slavery. The nineteenth century experienced a moral revulsion to slavery that was sufficiently strong to effect its abolition. It was on the wane in Britain and in South America, and it never really gained a foothold on the continent. Well before the overturn of so old and well entrenched an institution, there must be at first dormant, and then stirring with a long crescendo of activity, a set of attitudes that, when fully expressed, will be totally incompatible with the institution. The way in which most people will want to deal with such disquieting attitudes in their yet incipient state will be to let them sleep, and it may have been Webster's particular contribution to the comfort of his contemporaries that he devised themes and a style which combined to lull the stirring conscience of his country. It is significant that Emerson despised him, for Emerson stood for conscience above all else, and against slavery.

Slavery, of course, was a focal issue in nineteenth-century American public address, but it was not an autokinetic issue. A process of industrialization and technological development was under way in America and in England, a process that some historians believe put slavery in the course of economic extinction.[7] More important for our analysis, it was a process that, in both countries, created social disruption and human suffering. The god Progress reigned, and the salient tenet of its theology was to invest one's faith in the momentum of change. Faith in Progress required that one not be inhibited by social remorse. The accumulating detritus of the process—the ugliness, the exploitation, the social insecurities—all had to be accepted as an inevitable means to a higher good. What precisely the good was, was not clear, but the movement toward it required allegiance, and that allegiance in turn required that one's progress not be retarded by the suffering of others.

A form of consciousness emerged that was adapted to such demands, a form that was characterized by the subordination of moral to aesthetic considerations—by the achievement of psychic comfort and subcutaneous harmony through the refusal to apprehend the jarring, the unwholesome, the corrupt.

The themes of Hellenism and Hebraism in Matthew Arnold's great nineteenth-century essay were actual currents of his time, and it is by no means clear that Hellenism was not the dominant current in England and America, if by Hellenism we understand the impulse to subordinate moral to aesthetic claims.

There are at least two ways in which a society can express its preference for aesthetic values. One way is to beautify the environment, to adorn the civic life and the private domicile alike with ornaments and ostentation. The other way is to develop a perceptual instrument of highly discriminating selectivity, one that will be blind to the ugly and sensitive only to the beautiful. This sort of perceptual instrument can operate with indifference to the environment, and can realize Apollonian values without regard for what Marxists call "the objective conditions of society." But such a perceptual instrument has all the defects of its virtues, and its principal efficacy is its selective imperceptiveness. The instrument is required to be closed to some facts, even as it records others. Its failure to perceive is as important as its perceiving.

The development of such an instrument makes possible a Hellenism of the mind, an impulse to beautify that is never projected, a vision of the Good that is characteristically quiescent, an internal harmony in the midst of external squalor, an aesthetic anesthetic. At its crudest (and it was often crude in the nineteenth century) it is Pollyanna and all the other cloying sentimentalities that we associated with bourgois culture of the time; but it was not always crude, and sometimes it was a very subtly expressed disposition that enabled the elite of that century to abide the most extravagant corruptions and yet to maintain their consciences intact and guiltless.

When Freud wrote of the conscious mind as receiving material that had first passed through a censor, his insight was timelessly valuable, but the insight was of his age. Freud, the discoverer of the unconscious, was also a child of the nineteenth century, and his genius lay in his capacity to generalize from the evidence given him by his patients who, during the foundational formulation of his theory, were creatures of the nineteenth century. And Freud saw in that procession of troubled souls the recurrent configuration of a consciousness that protects itself by a willed ignorance of the ugly facts of its own nature, but an ignorance that, in the case of Freud's patients, was incompletely realized: successful enough to disguise the rot, but not successful enough to arrest the guilt. That Freud's therapeutic response was not to strengthen his patients' censors, but to throw open their psyches and bathe their guilt in light was what made Freud one of the prime adversaries of this nineteenth-century sensibility.

More courageously perhaps than any previous writer, Freud pressed the inquiry into the price we pay for civilization. His good faith brought him to acknowledge—as Rousseau before him had not—that the inquiry itself was an essentially cultural epiphenomenon, and that to pursue it was a profoundly civilized act. Freud demonstrated anew that the construction and sustenance of a civilization depends on hard moral choices, and that one can be free of such choices only in a state of savagery.

The pattern of personal anguish that Freud observed in the simultaneous presence of contradictory impulses crystallized, in the course of the nineteenth century, into a social configuration. Our civilization in that time had given our forebears the power to rape the earth, but it had also given them the moral apprehension of what they were doing. It sustained at once their arrogance and their humility and, having defined the two characteristics as irreconcilable, it sanctioned their anxiety about them. Our ancestors had, as we have still, a repertoire for coping with unendurable paradox, and one favorite technique of theirs was to obfuscate it, to befog it in sentimentality. They refined the use of language as an instrument not of rendering reality, but of obscuring it. They projected their wishes; they propagated their dreams. In their fortunate moments, they found an inconsequential solace and resolution. When their luck failed them, they were entrapped within the moral autonomy of their own fictions and perhaps, in time, they, or we their heirs, recovered from it as from a nightmare, then to look unsentimentally, remorsefully, even loathingly on the cruel achievements of their self-absorption.

The career of Oscar Wilde, and especially its tragic finale, is a particularly instructive example of the apotheosis of aesthetic values. Wilde's comedies and his public persona both carried to parodic extremes the pattern of so exalting the agreeable and the beautiful that they become perceptual filters. In the case of his comic masterpiece, *The Importance of Being Earnest*, for example, the pattern pervades the play and not only controls its plot and characterization, but also suffuses virtually all the wit. And even the moral tale "The Picture of Dorian Gray" is the story of a man whose corruption is disguised by an attractive appearance, and who might have flourished indefinitely but for a work of art—his portrait—that represented him too well. But it is Wilde's public persona even more strikingly than his writings—a public persona that was as successfully entertaining in this country as in England—that evidences our argument. If that argument has merit, then it requires us to see Wilde's public persona not as a decadent deviation, but rather as an especially pure embodiment of his time. It was typical of the century that the guardians of British prestige refused to see in Wilde's aestheticism the fulfillment of their own attitudes, for their own equivocation, being yet another source of moral discomfort, had itself to be a prime object of imperception.

The fury with which Wilde was pursued, hounded, and ruined has always been something of a perplexity to Wilde's biographers. They often end by holding Wilde himself responsible for his having suffered conviction and imprisonment rather than escaping into exile, as if a refusal to flee can account for the enmity that makes fleeing imperative in the first place.[8] Yet, for all the suggestions that a death wish in Wilde drove him to impudence, neither Wilde's career of fashionable impertinence nor his tactical paralysis in the face of Queensberry's accusations quite constitute an objective correlative to the relentless persecution that destroyed him. We can begin to appreciate the dynamism of that fury when we notice Wilde's relationship to the aestheticized morality of his time.

Wilde made overt in his art and, to all appearances, in his life as well the chronic disposition of the British elite to exalt their own tastes to a moral preeminence. By pushing as far as it would go—even into absurdity—the priority of aesthetic values over morality, Wilde was disclosing the secret allocations of his society. The prospect of that disclosure must have been frightening to the British establishment, for it opened to scrutiny and to critical review the delicate organization of their social consciousness. If they were brought to doubt the moral adequacy of aestheticism, their own sense of moral adequacy would, in the end, have been subverted, and they would have been forced to admit into the formal parlor of their consciences an ugly rabble of unacknowledged obligations.

In accounting for the destruction of Wilde, we cannot simply say that his sexual preferences repelled his society. Wilde did live a secret life, but not a singular one. His link to a hidden but flourishing world of night was unbearable to respectable Britons only because he was a special case. Wilde was vulnerable not because of his secret, but because of his disclosure. He had dared to project a hierarchy of values that gentility required be concealed, and to make his life illustrative of it.[9] His countrymen decided that he was a danger to their society, and they were right.

However unprepossessing a form of consciousness may be, however disreputable may be its stylistic symptoms, to attribute to it an epistemic function is to judge it as decisive and fateful in the lives of its adherents. Perceptual filters shape not simply the distinction between the real and unreal, but also, prior to that distinction, the very determination of what may or may not qualify as a subject for it.

The sentimental style is, among other things, symptomatic of a form of consciousness. It is the manifestation of a disposition to subordinate all values to aesthetic values. As such, it is the fallible sign of an evasion of moral responsibility. This style achieved an apogee, at least in Britain and America, in the nineteenth century. Since then, the style has fallen into disfavor, and on those rare occasions when we encounter it, it is likely to seem to us archaic and contrived.[10]

What has happened to the impulses behind this style? Surely our century has experienced neither a diminution of horrors to confront nor an enlargement of the appetite to confront them. We have no obvious reason to believe that the self-protectiveness of an aestheticized sensibility is any less useful now than it was before. One may suspect that the sentimental style has been replaced, that something else now exercises the close regulation of our responses in the way that the sentimental style once did. And the question is, What is that something else?

First, I think that we must look to television for part of the answer. In its reports and documentaries no less than in its soap operas and adventure stories, television subordinates its raw material to the demands of dramatic form. Unlike the sentimental style, television reportage and documentary do not seem to me to be shielding us from ugliness. On the contrary, they tend, if anything, to wallow in it. Television news presents a veritable plethora of moral concern, and we viewers are invited to live lives of unremitting social guilt. But even when it has horrors to convey, television orders, edits, and comments on its photography with strict attention to the dramaturgic expectations of its audience. Thus, television reportage works, as the sentimental style did, to render public issues aesthetically appealing.

More directly, we find a compressed version of the sentimental style in some television advertising: in the "morning in America" commercials that show laughing children and affectionate, white-haired elders or shimmering lakes and water birds in flight, each attractive image proximate to The Product. The values to which we are most unquestioningly faithful—values before which we may be consumed by sentiment—are, so the sponsors hope, being associated with products before which we may also be put into a consuming mood.

A second and more elusive answer to the question of what has happened to the sentimental style is suggested by the style's fashionable variability. The sentimental style is intrinsically transitory. Its effects eventually become incompatible with its functions.

To find how this occurs, we must put aside our focus on the evasive and circumventive functions of the sentimental style, and turn instead to its positive techniques. The sentimental style works by consolidating the perceptions that it sponsors with precisely defined feelings. The style, in effect, issues a series of imperative regulations of sentiment. And as those feelings are rehearsed in the auditor, and repeatedly associated with the same class of objects, those associations may become fixed, and thus qualify as pieties.

What begins in the sentimental style as the construction of a new sentiment can become, after a while, a stock response. It is an association that the auditor has assimilated; it has become part of a private repertoire of feelings, and at that point, its public exhibition may become repugnant. The repugnance is produced by two factors: One is the reluctance of people to submit to lessons in feeling that they have already learned. The other is the improbability that any representation of a private emotion will sufficiently correspond with the actual feeling of that emotion as to appear authentic. Hence, after the sentimental style has worked its effects on auditors, they may come to feel the style to be tedious and false. They will no longer find it persuasive because they have already been persuaded by it.

The melodrama of a hundred years ago, which was in technique and in effect a very exact theatrical counterpart of the sentimental style,[11] can become now the romance or the medical story or detective story of television and film. The modern entertainments are cooler and more implicative in style, but are able to function only because the amalgams of object and emotion that the older drama made explicit have by now become constituents of our conventional sensibility, and what had to be taught to our forebears may be simply evoked in us.

The sentimental style is transitory because it is always, when it is effectual, at a threshold in the formation or deformation of fundamental attitudes. It is a style that compensates for a deficiency of confidence in the appropriate relations between attitudes and conditions. It burgeons most in three general circumstances: when a new sensibility is taking form to replace an older one; when a sensibility has become competitively marginal to an alternative; and when an established sensibility is in decline. In any of those three circumstances and because of any of those circumstances some version of the sentimental style may appear. Depending on the particular circumstance, the style may work either to instruct new initiates or to renew the faithful. But to an audience not in any of those circumstances, the sentimental style will be boring and overdone. It will not flourish because they will not attend it.

This inquiry has concerned some relations between a style and a form of consciousness. The consideration of significant form in rhetorical criticism is usually directed to recurrent patterns in discourses. That focus is indispensable. There is, however, another locus of form that solicits attention, one that is more elusive than discursive form because it is less directly observable. It is the form of consciousness affected by and manifested in the symbolic currency of rhetorical transactions.

Groups of people often become distinctive as groups by their habitual patterns of commitment—not by the beliefs they hold, but by the manner in which they hold them and give them expression. Such people do not necessarily share ideas. Rather, they share stylistic proclivities and the qualities of mental life of which those proclivities are tokens.

The varieties of rhetorical experience are complexedly layered and interconnected. Below the mercurial dialectic that shapes and reshapes our social actions, there are deeper continuities of form. Beyond beliefs are the configurations of belief.

5
Authoritarian Fiction

————— Susan Warner's novel *The Wide, Wide World* has been called by Jane Tompkins, a prominent feminist critic, "the Ur-text of the nineteenth-century United States."[1] Tompkins writes of it, "The book remains compulsively readable, absorbing, and provoking to an extraordinary degree."[2]

In the laudable effort to reassess our received opinions of literature—an exercise that should be continuous—and to retrieve from historical neglect works that have been denied their appropriate consideration because of the operation of illegitimate prejudices, Tompkins has advanced *The Wide, Wide World* as a candidate for canonical exaltation.[3] My disagreement with Tompkins's judgment of this novel's quality is of no more significance than I hold the novel itself to be, except that some of the issues attending that disagreement may be germane to a larger consideration of the sentimental style. That a rhetorical critic should address issues pertaining to a work of fiction is a result of the strongly didactic—the rhetorical—nature of the work, a characterization of the novel that Tompkins has herself persuasively argued.

The Wide, Wide World was first published in 1850. It went through fourteen editions in two years, and sold more copies than any novel ever had in the history of the United States.

Its popularity was equally great in Britain. It was, in fact, one of the best-selling novels in the English language of the century. As Tompkins indicates in her afterword to a recent edition of the book, it was extravagantly praised in some of the most august journals of the day. Indeed, no less an eminence than Henry James compared its realism favorably to Flaubert's. It is not recorded what Flaubert thought of that comparison.

The Wide, Wide World is the story of Ellen Montgomery, a nine-year-old girl at the beginning of the novel, a young woman—perhaps in her late teens—at its end. It is the story of Ellen's sufferings, her endurance, and above all, of her progress toward the fulfillment of a Christian ideal.

Initially the focus of the novel is on Ellen's relationship with her ailing mother. It is a relationship of unbounded love, but it is shadowed by the mother's illness, an illness—the reader learns—that is to be mortal. Because of financial reversals and the precarious health of the mother, a decision is taken by the father—a dim and unsympathetic figure in this novel—to take her with him to Europe and to place Ellen temporarily with a paternal aunt whom she has never met. The aunt proves a cold, mean woman whose rural household is crude and austere by the standards that little Ellen has experienced. In the course of time, Ellen develops significant relations with others, especially Alice and John Humphreys, sister and brother, with whom Ellen becomes intensely involved. After the death of Alice, Ellen takes up residence in the Humphreys house and comes under the religious tutelage of John, who is a devout young minister. There are various reversals of Ellen's fortunes and tests of her character before, in the end, she marries John and the two of them settle in for what the reader is encouraged to believe will be lives of piety and affluence.

So brief a summary scarcely begins to inventory the characters that appear in this lengthy work, but in a sense, the novel itself makes such an inventory superfluous. Its characters are consolidated into two types, making their individual differentiation at once more difficult and less purposive. The two types are: good and bad. The good characters are those who have accepted or are in the course of accepting Jesus as their savior. The bad characters—and they are not numerous in this novel—are those who are occupied with other matters. Only one character, a minor one named Nancy, makes a transition from bad to better. Yet, paradoxically, despite the crushing simplification of character that the novel sponsors, it is, if it is anything, a novel of character. It satisfies all the formal requirements of the bildungsroman.

I have already alluded to two conditions of this work that contribute to its sentimentality: first, it focuses on character while, at the same time, it simplifies character; and second, its virtuous characters are much more numerous and prominently presented than its tainted characters. Let us reflect briefly on those properties.

The simplification of character is not unprecedented in fiction. Sonya, a pivotal character in *Crime and Punishment*, displays a simplicity that is accentuated by its contrast to Raskolnikov's complexity. But we are made to know what has brought Sonya to this condition of simplicity; we are made to know what experiences and what choices have shaped her life to the saintly condition that at last she attains.

In *The Wide, Wide World*, by contrast, characters are introduced with their moral qualities already assigned. They are not drawn in ways that imply personal histories: they are neither eccentric nor mysterious. They simply are there, most of them given pieties to mouth that are designed to be straightforward revelations of their inner lives. The actions that they are represented as taking are stereotypically conventional for the place, time, class, and occupation assigned them. Only Nancy—the single morally transitional character referred to earlier—commits anything that can be regarded as an impetuous act; but Warner did not become Miltonically enchanted with her morally ambiguous creation. The centerpiece of the novel is, steadfastly, sweet little Ellen.

This postulation of the narrowest variety of character types that is possible—two, good and bad—is a simplification that constitutes a necessary condition for sentimentality. Complexity of character in turn requires complexity of response from the reader, and so loosens the affective control that is at

the heart of sentimentality. Consider, for example, the following passage:

> Ellen was sure, indeed, from the way in which Mr.
> Humphreys [the aged father of John and the now-
> dead Alice] spoke to her, looked at her, now and
> then laid his hand on her head, and sometimes,
> very rarely, kissed her forehead, that he loved her
> and loved to see her about; and that her wish of
> supplying Alice's place was in some little measure
> fulfilled. Few as those words and looks were, they
> said more to Ellen than whole discourses would
> from other people; the least of them gladdened her
> heart with the feeling that she was a comfort to
> him. But she never knew how much. Deep as the
> gloom still over him was, Ellen never dreamed
> how much deeper it would have been, but for the
> little figure flitting round and filling up the va-
> cancy; how much he reposed on the gentle look of
> affection, the pleasant voice, the watchful thought-
> fulness that never left any thing undone that she
> could do for his pleasure. (Pp. 460–61)

The work of the passage is characterization. It is a dyadic
characterization. We are to deepen our understanding of Ellen and, to a lesser extent, of Mr. Humphreys by observing
their interaction. In this passage, she is active, he is passive.
Her behavior toward him is generalized. It is not depicted—
the account is too abstract to be called a depiction. We are
given, by references to her "gentle look of affection . . . pleasant voice . . . watchful thoughtfulness" not a concrete account of specific actions, but generalizations about his perceptions of her actions. His attitude toward her, however, is
manifested in his actions. He "spoke to her, looked at her . . .
laid his hand on her head . . . kissed her forehead." The central focus of the passage, then, is on Ellen's character, and two
means are employed to portray it. One is a concrete depiction, through the presentation of his actions, of Mr. Humphreys's attitude toward her; and the other is an abstract account of some of her characteristics, especially as they
impinge on and warrant Mr. Humphreys's attitude. More

specifically, we readers are to accept Mr. Humphreys's attitudes toward Ellen—however dim they may be—as our own. Mr. Humphreys is the medium through which we are to be persuaded of Ellen's virtuousness. Technically, the only way of achieving this form of persuasion is to make the medium— in this passage, the Humphreys character—completely reliable.

The technique produces a dual effect on the reader. The vehicular character—Mr. Humphreys—is apprehended as simple. And the tenor character—Ellen—is apprehended as distanced. These difficulties of apprehension, associated with this technique, could be overcome if we were to learn of one character through the narrative of another; but in this passage, and throughout *The Wide, Wide World,* the articulation of an internal state is accomplished through conventionally expressive conduct—most frequently, weeping—which invites a stock response in the reader, or through detached generalization, which solicits, at most, a tepid and ill-defined response from the reader.

The passage contains in miniature the strategy of the whole novel. It compresses the inferential latitude of the reader. Instead of encountering depictions of action that constitute a body of evidence from which the reader may imagine the actors' internal states, the reader encounters either determinative descriptions of internal states or the representation of prejudicial responses to them. The reader has nothing to decide except whether to continue being a reader.

The characters in the novel in whose reactions we see Ellen reflected are uniformly uncomplicated. Their motives are pure and transparent. The reader is not required to identify with such characters, but only to suspend disbelief, which is an easy task because there is nothing in the characterizations per se that would generate disbelief. To require the reader to interpret a character ironically—to discount a character's testimony except when the unreliability of that testimony was blatant—to exercise a subtle skepticism, would be to induce in the reader a convictional condition that is exactly contrary to that being advanced. In place of faith, we would have doubt; in place of rigid self-discipline, we would have an opening of multivalent possibilities; in place of aestheticized perceptions, we would entertain the prospect of multifarious motives and ambiguous intentions. We would, in sum, cultivate in the reader a state of mind with the capacity for incredulity: a state of mind incompatible with the rigorously perpetuated innocence that, in the character of Ellen, is advanced as the cynosure of Christian morality.

Another requisite for sentimentality is supplied by the novel's being dominated by the good characters. Villains make only rare appearances in *The Wide, Wide World*. For most of its pages, we are reading of simple, good people talking to one another of their simple goodness. These are the conditions that give the novel a saccharine quality. Reading it, indeed, is an experience akin to being submerged in treacle.

Unsurprisingly, a Victorian prudery is evident in the novel's omissions. Although the story concerns a period of perhaps ten years in the life of its central character, and although most of those ten years are set in the kind of farming area where, in real life, animals are bred and human beings multiply, nowhere in the novel's space does there appear an infant, there are no pregnancies, and the only wedding that occurs is barren. Once Ellen happens upon a calf on her aunt's farm; another time she is shown some kittens. There is nothing of birth, nothing of procreation. If a visitor from another planet had no knowledge of earth other than what it could glean from this novel, the report taken back to Venus would be that earthlings die, they yearn to die, they talk incessantly of dying, but yet they are not born. Their only pleasures are contemplative and the surfaces below their waists are evidently smooth.

They are not, however, unemotional. There are tears on nearly every page of the novel. Tears are, indeed, the only bodily secretion even remotely suggested, but their volume forms a veritable Niagara. Ellen's weeping is so copious and frequent that a sympathetic reader could become concerned about her possible dehydration. But she is not alone in this liquidity. The other female characters, too, are quick to join Ellen in shedding tears, in scenes that represent a recurrent epidemic of weeping throughout the novel. Male characters too, although represented as less demonstrative than the females, occasionally and with the utmost discretion allow themselves to contribute to the incessant drenching that marks—one is tempted to say, watermarks—this book.

Tears are shed at times of sadness, of course. But weeping also accompanies moments of joy or of enlightenment or of disappointment. In fact, weeping is prompted by virtually any emotion at all. Crying, in this novel, has two semantic functions. First, it signifies that the character who is weeping is experiencing an emotion. While that observation is admittedly not penetrating, it concerns a work that is less than profound. The second function of weeping, closely tied to the first, is that it signals the character's sincerity. The reader is to become convinced, whenever a character sheds tears, that the character is having an ingenuous moment, that the authenticity of the character's internal state has overwhelmed the character's reserve or capacity to dissemble, and that tears are the compulsive expression of this genuine emotion.

Now all of this sobbing and wailing would be only passingly notable—perhaps as a symptom of the meager expressive armamentarium of the novelist—except for one interesting fact. There was at large in the middle of the nineteenth century a variety of therapeutic theories, called "nature religions." These theories, which governed the acquisition and maintenance of good health, included hydropathy, homeopathy, and, later, chiropractic, among others, and they were commonly informed by a hydrostatic metaphor—an image of the mind or of energy or of the body's organs acting fluidly. Two eighteenth-century visionaries had supplied the foundations of these theories: Emanuel Swedenborg, whose notion of a "divine influx" in the natural world complemented the "magnetic tides" postulated by Franz Anton Mesmer.[4]

That same hydrostatic metaphor appeared later in the nineteenth century in a therapeutic theory that is still with us: that of Sigmund Freud, whose vision—of a precariously channeled and ceaselessly turbulent id that may breach its main and engulf the ego—can be said, in more senses than one, to plumb the depths of the mind. We have, then, not simply a manifestation of sentimentality in the novel's numerous scenes of weeping; we have, in addition, a mode of behavior assigned to characters that links with a much more general and pervasive attitude of the nineteenth century, an attitude associated with, of all things, fluids.

There is more: The great points of transition that mark Ellen's progress in the novel are presented as voyages by sea. When she is torn from the bosom of her dying mother to be thrust into the emotionally stingy guardianship of her aunt, the passage occurs in the form of a voyage during which Ellen is in the care of an old harridan whose psychological cruelty anticipates "aunt Fortune." In a later scene, which recapitulates Ellen's earlier orphaning, when she is compelled to leave the sanctity of the Humphreys house and live with her anti-American relatives in Scotland, a trip on water signals the transition. Ellen's mother departs from her by water, and her father's death is by drowning. Her beloved spiritual tutor, John, takes his longest and most painful absence from Ellen when he voyages by ship. All of the wrenching separations in the novel are associated either with water or with death.

But water does not appear only in melancholy transitions. Other lamentable circumstances are also dank: In her initial encounter with Nan, a malicious girl who is eventually rehabilitated by Ellen's piety, Nan's mischief is displayed by her causing Ellen to fall into water. At least twice in the novel, the meanness of aunt Fortune's house is signaled by Ellen's access to bath water. She must use a crude arrangement that provides only chilled water for her to bathe in. Fortune has not provided Ellen with water that is warm.

Indeed, a critic under the influence of Otto Rank, whose pioneering doctrines sought the feminization of psychoanalytic theory,[5] could make a tolerably good case that this sodden novel is "really" occupied with the birth trauma, and that the appearance of water as a precursive signal of that trauma is, everywhere in the novel, an unconscious manifestation of its true theme. Moreover, the event that sets the plot going—Ellen's separation from her mother—is supremely consonant with that theme, as is Ellen's arduous rebirth as a true Christian. The Rankian critic could even, by squinting just right, see in the voyages by sea an implied pun, pregnant with nascent significance, made possible by the homophonic "naval" and "navel." And the Rankian critic could, with a final flourish, link the novel to its author by noting that the woman who, in an act of autogenous conception, drew this novel out of herself—who created the child, Ellen—experienced in the process the closest she was ever known to have come to parturition; that her breaking water with a flood upon this work may have signified to her, at least, a laboring and bringing forth.

We have, then, in Ellen's tears and those of the other characters, in trips by water that mark important changes in the main character's condition, in dunkings that are uniformly uncomfortable for the heroine (she never is described as experiencing a pleasant soak), and in the fluid metaphors that pervaded nineteenth-century nature religions a set of clues concerning one structure of imagery important to this novel.

One way of interpreting this imagistic saturation would be to note that the author spent most of her life living on an island in the Hudson River, an island that her father had tried to own, but had lost. Surrounded as she was by water, it seems natural that her conception of the world would be—if I may be permitted—watercolored. Because of financial misfortunes that her father had suffered a few years before she wrote *The Wide, Wide World*, Warner's experience was still vivid of the possibility of that island being controlled, possessed, owned, subordinated to a will; but that patch of ground—a property that could be turned to a human purpose or used to disappoint one—was surrounded by a restless, roiling, uncontrollable force, an element both familiar and mysterious, a river relentless as time itself. The river, the ocean, the tear on the cheek of the child—all represented something beyond arrangement, beyond regulation.

Diluted as the image may be, water is one of the merely two recurrent elements of the novel that are outside its constricting moral order. The fluids are beyond control; the liquids are free, responding solely to the amoral laws of physics. The only other unconstrained force, appearing briefly in the novel, is a cat, but a creature that—although referred to twice as an "unconscious" being—is still endowed with scruples and is made capable of giving and receiving affection. Still, it is a creature obedient to its feline proclivities; it is tamed and domesticated, but it is without the circle of convictions that this novel sponsors as guides and inhibitions.

Weeping is the first, the most primitive, the most infantile of human expressions. Before the baby has any medium of communication, before it has the capacity to distinguish among its wants, it proclaims its undifferentiated distress in crying and tears. The novelist's repeated exploitation of that single, pristine signal represents more than simply an impoverished authorial repertoire—although it certainly represents that. Tears of shame, of remorse, and of embarrassment can also be associated with the substantive view of religion that this novel—which is really a religious tract—sustains. That view is most clearly revealed in the scene in which our little Ellen first encounters Alice Humphreys, the young woman who is to become her surrogate sister. Ellen is alone on a hillside, weeping convulsively. Alice comes upon her and asks, sympathetically, why she is crying. Ellen replies, between sobs, that she intended to be a good child, but had been a bad one. Alice asks for an explanation. Ellen says:

> I will tell you ma'am. That first day I left mamma—
> when I was on board the steamboat and feeling as
> badly as I could feel, a kind, kind gentleman, I
> don't know who he was, came to me and spoke to
> me, and took care of me the whole day. Oh, if I
> could see him again! He talked to me a great deal;
> he wanted me to be a Christian; he wanted me to
> make up my mind to begin that day to be one; and
> ma'am, I did. I did resolve with my whole heart,
> and I thought I should be different from that time
> from what I had ever been before. But I think I
> have never been so bad in my life as I have been
> since then. Instead of feeling right I have felt
> wrong all the time, almost,—and I can't help it. I
> have been passionate and cross, and bad feelings
> keep coming, and I know it's wrong, and it makes
> me miserable. And yet, oh! ma'am, I haven't
> changed my mind a bit,—I think just the same as I
> did that day; I want to be a Christian more than

any thing else in the world, but I am not,—and
what shall I do! (P. 151)

Alice and Ellen kneel together and pray, after which Alice ad-
vises Ellen that prayer and Bible reading are the solutions to
her problem.

Note what that problem is: "Instead of feeling right I have
felt wrong all the time. . . . I have been passionate and cross,
and bad feelings keep coming."

The message of this novel is squarely in the center of the
evangelical tradition, which conceives of Christianity as
preeminently a governance of feelings. It is not primarily a
code of conduct; only derivatively does it regulate behavior.
The passage that I have quoted, as the whole of this novel, is
advocating a psychological regime: a credo that, although
grounded in cosmology, is essentially designed to regulate
the quality and character of the inner life.

Under such a regime, a provocation for weeping is imma-
terial. Just as the crying infant knows only its own woe, but
not the reasons thereof, so it is sufficient for Ellen, and for
Susan Warner's chosen reader as well, to know only that Ellen's internal state is yet imperfect. Weeping tells us only that;
but in the terms of this novel, that is enough. It is, as I have
mentioned, a religious tract, but one with a shriveled conception of religion, especially by the spiritually impassioned
standards of its time.

While piety is omnipresent in the novel, God is absent.
That is to say, there is nothing in the novel, nothing in any of
its events or characterizations to suggest, even remotely, a
spiritual power that acts upon the world. Ellen is urged to
have faith, she is persuaded to a condition of spiritual longing, she is importuned to pray and be watchful, but her
yearnings are cast into an unanswering void. The reader witnesses no indication of a supernal intrusion into the affairs of
the world, no transcendental potentialities in human beings,
no episode of spiritual awakening. Even the bearers of the sacred word are without charisma. They are kindly, patient, and
self-possessed, exhibiting that restraint and discipline that is,
in this novel, the object of Christian endeavor; but the events

of the novel are affected neither by revelation nor by divine intervention. The deity is a Great Absence. The focus of the novel is undeviatingly on the regulation of internal states.

We are rehearsed in the conditions of readiness for divine intervention, but we are not brought beyond those preparatory efforts. On the evidence of the novel, revelation is not its concern. An alternative concern supervenes, and it is psychological rather than metaphysical. The central gravamen of this didactic novel has to do with the proper shaping of the internal life, not with the visionary rewards that sanctify that proper shaping.

As if to reinforce this doctrine, those scenes in the novel in which the moral value of overt conduct, as against internal condition, is at issue present moral dilemmas of suffocating triviality. Here are the instances of Ellen's misconduct: she says "ain't" and misuses the word "fix"; she becomes engrossed in a book and loses track of time; she reads *Blackwood's Magazine;* she is reluctant in agreeing to be the regular amanuensis, gratis, for an illiterate man.

It is odd and striking that her acts of misconduct, although rare, are all connected to language, to reading, writing, or speaking. Perhaps here we are getting a clue that the author has identified herself with her character. But more important is the significance of these acts, or rather, their insignificance. They are petty; they are inconsequential; and yet, they receive concentrated attention in the novel. Each misdeed is followed by a sanctimonious admonition from John, who is the font of religious verity, and then by a paroxysm of remorse from Ellen, characteristically expressed in weeping.

The moral triviality of the novel accomplishes two ends. The first, as has been mentioned, is to reinforce the doctrine that it is the inner state, not the outward act, that merits the highest moral priority. The second is to establish that this doctrine does not and cannot support an intelligent perspective on morality; it cannot render any but the grossest kinds of distinctions among modes of behavior.

In 1929, H. L. Mencken published a brief essay in the *American Mercury* about a scandalous murder that had occurred two years before. Henry Judd Gray, a respectable and pious corset salesman with a wife and children, had taken up an affair with Ruth Brown Snyder. Together they murdered Mrs. Snyder's husband. The two of them confessed the crime, and were executed in 1928. Why did the holy-minded Henry Judd Gray participate in murder? Mencken's answer was that once Gray had entered into his affair with Mrs. Snyder, he was without further moral inhibitions because he regarded himself as doomed to hell anyhow. Not even the divine omnipotence can further prolong a damnation that is already eternal.

Gray's view was similar to that which informs this novel. And my point is similar to Mencken's: The effect of centering morality on the character of the inner life is to trivialize the morality of behavior.

An illustration of this moral trivialization occurs in a brief scene between Ellen and Mrs. Vawse, a sympathetically drawn older character. Ellen confronts a moral dilemma: A letter from her late mother, newly revealed, has instructed Ellen to travel to Edinburgh and to take up residence with her formerly estranged grandmother. But prior to the discovery of the letter, Ellen had promised her dying friend, Alice, to remain in Alice's household and to look after Alice's aged father. Which duty should Ellen perform? Should she obey her late mother's injunction? Or should she keep her promise to her dead friend? The matter requires less than a page to dispatch in the scene between Ellen and Mrs. Vawse. Mrs. Vawse speaks:

> "You must do what is *right;* and you know it cannot be but that will be the best and happiest for you in the end."
>
> "Oh, I wish—I wish," exclaimed Ellen from the bottom of her heart,—"those letters had never been found!"
>
> "Nay, Ellen, *that* is not right."
>
> "But I promised Alice, Mrs. Vawse; ought I go away and leave him? Oh, Mrs. Vawse, it is very hard! *Ought* I?"
>
> "Your father and your mother have said it, my child."
>
> "But they never would have said it if they had known?"

"But they did not know, Ellen; and here it is."
Ellen wept violently. . . . (P. 493)

This scene is typical of the novel in several important ways that bear on the sentimental style. The focus of the scene is not on a moral dilemma. It is, rather, on Ellen's ambivalence; or, more exactly, on the unacceptability of Ellen's inclination to respect her promise to Alice—a judgment authorized by Mrs. Vawse, a character whom the novel represents as having practical wisdom (*phronesis*). The reader is not allowed the instructive experience of witnessing a struggle of conscience. Rather, the reader is made to observe the correction of an impulse that, however moral-appearing, is subsidiary to a contravening obligation. The possibility that there may actually be an interesting moral dilemma latent in Ellen's situation is not suggested by the novel. The reader can become aware of that possibility only by drawing an inference that is independent of the code governing the novel.

Ellen's duty is to obey her mother's injunction, as Mrs. Vawse unequivocally maintains. Has Ellen any obligation to keep her promise to Alice? She is given words consistent with thinking so, but presumably because the Bible commands filial piety, Mrs. Vawse—a source of truth and rectitude—does not even acknowledge the existence of a dilemma, never mind explore one. There is a right, and Mrs. Vawse knows it. Duty is duty: blind to circumstance, indifferent to consequences. Duty may cause a variety of pains, but the anxiety of ambivalence is not one of them. Ellen is not challenged to struggle for a moral judgment, and—more important—neither is the reader, even vicariously.

The passivity that this scene cultivates in the reader is reinforced by its cliches ("the bottom of her heart," "Ellen wept violently"). They work as verbal rivulets, flowing smoothly through well-worn indentations on the surface of the reader's consciousness. Nothing impedes them: neither denial, nor doubt, nor assent, nor even rapt attention. They soothingly contribute to a condition of pliant, gullible inertness. If we could imagine a catatonic capable of attending to a text, we would have envisioned the ideal product of the rhetorical forces deployed by this novel.

Jane Tompkins's defense of the novel includes the assertion "that Warner's heroine cannot be dismissed because she *is* us" (p. 597, italics in original). It is certainly possible to understand why a critic could find interest in this novel as a feminist text. Its central character is a girl, subjected to the rigorous discipline of a Victorian code, shaped to a life of subordination. In the novel's earliest scenes, the father of Ellen displays coarseness and insensitivity and arrogance; the mother displays foresight, sympathy, and courage. He has many of the traditionally masculine vices; she has most of the traditionally feminine virtues. They both are helpless to prevent or to cure the mother's tragic illness, but they do not respond equally well to that testing.

Tompkins's feminist interpretation of the novel requires that she focus her remarks on its central character, Ellen, and scant other female characters that will not easily fit her interpretation. For example, Ellen's aunt, who is the father's half sister, displays some of the same authoritarian callousness of the father, and in the end, the reader is left to infer that this insensitivity may be more attributable to genes than to gender. There are other female characters—Mrs. Vawse has already been mentioned—who, more benignly than the aunt, display strength and independence, who cannot be apprehended as the "vulnerable, powerless and innocent" victims that a feminist interpretation requires.

Tompkins is compelled to concede on the page immediately following her claim that "[Ellen] *is* us" that "*The Wide, Wide World* draws us irresistibly and intimately into the mind of a character who affirms and acts on beliefs that, in many respects, violate our innermost sense of what a human being can be." (Never mind the logical problem of holding that we *are* a character whose beliefs we find repugnant.) Far from being drawn "into the mind of a character"—a reification of dubious critical utility—we are presented by this novel with only the most superficial portraits. As the typical scene quoted above illustrates, the emotional range of the novel is extremely attenuated, in keeping with its imposition on the reader of paradigms of moral choice that are paltry and unworthy of attention. The novel sustains an antiseptic conception of human experience.

Before we too hastily follow Tompkins in consigning the defects of this work to the constraints of its time, let us remind ourselves that the author of this "Ur-text" was a contemporary of Melville and Dostoyevski and Dickens and Thackeray, of George Eliot and the Brontë sisters. She lived after Hawthorne and Longfellow and Cooper, after Mary Shelly, after Jane Austen.

Tompkins writes, "More than any other book of its time, it embodies, uncomprisingly, the values of the Victorian era" (p. 585). It was the time, as well, of the queen's favorite prime minister, Benjamin Disraeli, whose embodiment of values was deeply prized by the woman who gave the era its name, and who wrote novels abundant in the qualities that Warner's book so conspicuously lacks: wit and complexity and moral subtlety.[6]

The Wide, Wide World is a novel that exhibits sentimentality thematically as well as formally. Elsewhere I have argued that the sentimental style is characterized by its close regulation of responses. The sentimental style is one that creates no ambiguities, and that leaves no room for the auditor or reader to construct an affective reaction. It is a style marked by the effort to spell out, in the minutest detail possible, every shade and nuance of feeling that the auditor is to experience in engagement with the work. My example was some of the more florid epideictic oratory of Daniel Webster, who was flourishing at the time of this novel, and an apposite example it was. *The Wide, Wide World*, however, is an even clearer case of functional sentimentality.

The absolute control over Ellen's inner life that religious doctrine is supposed to have corresponds in its dominance to the control that the novel seeks over its reader. The novel leaves no room for the reader's imagination, no room for the reader's construction of experience, no room for the reader's participation. The novel demands a reader with the temperament of an ox and the intellect of a zombie. Every page constructs and constricts the reaction appropriate to it, and while that is certainly not a procedure uncommon to fiction, it is the extreme compression of the permitted response that makes the sentimental style extraordinary.

The control over response that the novel exercises leaves it airless and overdetermined. Those qualities, as well as a representative sample of its prose, are especially evident in an early scene involving Ellen and her mother. The mother, preparing for her separation from Ellen, has given Ellen a sewing kit, whose contents Ellen inventories and savors as a miser would inventory and savor a hoard of gold.

> Ellen joyfully allotted the whole morning to the examination and trial of her new possessions; and as soon as breakfast was over and the room clear she set about it. She first went through the desk and every thing in it, making a running commentary on the excellence, fitness, and beauty of all it contained; then the dressing-box received a share, but a much smaller share, of attention; and lastly, with fingers trembling with eagerness she untied the packthread that was wound round the work-box, and slowly took off cover after cover; she almost screamed when the last was removed. The box was of satin-wood, beautifully finished, and lined with crimson silk; and Mrs. Montgomery had taken good care it should want nothing that Ellen might need to keep her clothes in perfect order.
>
> "Oh, mamma, how beautiful! Oh, mamma, how good you are! Mamma, I promise you I'll never be a slattern. Here is more cotton than I can use up in a great while—every number, I do think; and needles, oh, the needles! what a parcel of them! and, mamma! what a lovely scissors! did you choose it, mamma, or did it belong to the box?"
>
> "I chose it."
>
> "I might have guessed it, mamma, it's just like you. And here's a thimble—fits me exactly; and an emery-bag! how pretty!—and a bodkin! this is a great deal nicer than yours, mamma—yours is decidedly the worse for wear;—and what's this?— Oh, to make eyelet holes with, I know. And oh, mamma! here is almost every thing, I think—here are tapes, buttons, and hooks and eyes, and darning cotton, and silk-winders, and pins, and all sorts of things. What's this for, mamma?"

"That's a scissors to cut button-holes with. Try it
on that piece of paper that lies by you, and you will
see how it works."

"Oh, I see!" said Ellen, "how very nice that is.
Well, I shall take great pains now to make my
button-holes very handsomely."

One survey of her riches could by no means satisfy Ellen. For some time she pleased herself with
going over and over the contents of the box, finding each time something new to like. At length she
closed it, and keeping it still in her lap, sat awhile
looking thoughtfully into the fire; till turning toward her mother she met her gaze, fixed mourn-
fully, almost tearfully, on herself. The box was in-
stantly shoved aside, and getting up and bursting
into tears, Ellen went to her. "Oh, dear mother,"
she said, "I wish they were all back in the store, if I
could only keep you." (Pp. 40–41)

It is as if the contraction of the reader's range of responses
had become generalized into a condensation of the characters' as well. Ellen must withhold her impulses because they
are likely to be wicked, which leads to a general withholding,
which leads in turn to an anal-retentive savoring of the withheld. There is no play here or elsewhere, no play either in the
sense of frolic or in the sense of space for movement. Not
even the scenes of celebration are endowed with spontaneity;
they are formalistic social minuets. Everything is grim, rigid,
fastened down, restrained by prescriptions. That is true of
the characters, with the solitary exception of Nancy, the morally transitional one; and the novel's animus is, in the end, to
make it true of the reader as well. The novel makes tension
pervasive. The mind of the reader is to go in only one direction; its impulses, vagrancies, imaginings are to be checked.
The novel has a message and that message is: control, submit,
withhold: the clinched mouth, the bowed head, the taut
sphincter. Weeping is the sole release permitted.[7]

It is difficult to determine whether the sentimental style is
based on confidence or fear. When one has the truth and is
secure in the conviction of having it, then the creation of ambiguity or the multiplication of epistemic choice is either a fri-
volity or a betrayal of the auditor. There is nothing to do but

so to frame the delivery of truth that it is exact and undeniable. That impulse to restrict the response of the auditor would originate in confidence. On the other hand, the gnawing fear that the auditor lacks the moral or intellectual capacity to acknowledge a presented truth is also a component of the inclination to the sentimental style. There is, behind the style, a rejection of ambiguity, a wish to attenuate the options available to an interlocutor, an exercise of authority over effect.

We may find reflected in the sentimental style the confidence of a past age, a confidence in dogmas that had not yet been undermined by the skepticism of science or the disillusion of wars. But we may also find implicit in the sentimental style doubts about the appeal of those dogmas, misgivings concerning the will or the ability of an audience freely to accept them.

A distinction fundamental to the discipline of rhetoric is the distinction between persuasion and coercion. The sentimental style situates itself on the indeterminate boundary between the two, and often, in the explicitness of its instructions concerning response and in its exclusion of any range or variation of effect except the typically blatant ones that it sponsors, the sentimental style substitutes duress for inducement.

Consider the condition of the Roman who, in 1936, is packed into the crowd in the square, surrounded by police who forbid him to leave for any reason, and baked under the hot sun for two or three hours, waiting for Il Duce.[8] At last, the great man appears on the balcony above, and discharges an oration to which cheering is the only permitted response. Preliminarily, through physical restriction and systematic debilitation, the Roman's mind is cleared. He is kneaded into a condition in which his only thought is of his pressing discomfort, and the reaction to which he is most prone is one of gratitude upon seeing his deliverer—Mussolini—finally appear and begin the harangue that will orchestrate the Roman's catharsis of his pent-up distress. The oration's impressions on an exhausted and ill-used auditor are striking. They fill his mind completely; he is incapable of considering any alternative to them or of subjecting them to any psychological resistance. Later perhaps, rested and quiet, he may be able to reflect on what he has heard. Later he may recover an aptitude for skepticism. But the discourse will have gained a presumption in his mind. He will have attended it with a reinvigorated intensity; he will have associated it with a release of tension and with a gratifying surrender of himself. He will have experienced a rhetorical equivalent of fascism.

Although it is true that print cannot have the immediacy of speech, that the requisition of a response is beyond the capacity of a book, and that a reader is free at any moment to terminate an engagement with a text and cease being a reader, nonetheless the sentimental style is a moderated version of the same generic form that, in its extremity, is illustrated by the ill-used Roman. The sentimental style is, to use a term especially dear to current criticism, hegemonic: it functions to establish its own deliberately narrowed sensibilities within its auditors, to the exclusion of all else. When the sentimental style is the subject of a transitory engagement—as it almost always is in the act of reading a novel—then its potential influence is equally transitory. You make yourself malleable for an hour, and become an automaton for that hour, and then come back into yourself. You give yourself up temporarily to a passive recreation. But let us be clear in understanding the character of that harmless experience. You have taken a nontoxic taste of totalitarianism. You have experienced something that mind-doctors of various persuasions have sought, indeed are seeking now, to make permanent in their prescriptions for one or another ideological regime. There is no gainsaying the political component of that style. Indeed, its political component is the most interesting thing about it. It is a style that brooks no opposition, no deviation, no variety; it insists on the totality of itself.

A surrender to sentimentality does not necessarily lead to totalitarianism; in fact, it very seldom does. Literary sentimentality is one of those narcoses, among the countless narcoses that are available to us, that tempts us, that we occasionally savor, but that in the end we have not the appetite or patience to endure. It is a temporary fix; an escapist interlude. So, a given instance of the sentimental style may have no discernible political consequences. But consequential or not, the sentimental style has an intrinsic political character.

There is a model of rhetorical activity that stands in polar contrast to the sentimental style. That model is an Emersonian ideal which envisions a self-determining auditor, with a rich inventory of political convictions intact, encountering a new idea. And that Emersonian auditor rejects or assimilates or modifies that new idea under the discipline of that inventory of settled convictions. If the auditor adopts the idea in any form, its integration into the auditor's body of belief will correspond to Eliot's account of the effect that the reception of a new masterpiece has on the history of literature. The idea will produce a subtle accommodation among all the old convictions. The Emersonian auditor will comprehend the old convictions in a new way and in new relationships, affected by their new member. But whatever its effects, the rhetorical transaction will be an encounter between a formed and freely choosing consciousness and a new claim that has been made upon it. This Emersonian model represents, perhaps, the purest possible conception of a free and individuated rhetorical act.

The sentimental style is the instrument of a different sort of encounter, one in which a subject yields totally to the demands of the style, suspends or abandons previous convictions, expurgates all competing or distracting ideas, surrenders to the text. That is the totalitarian model.

We should not fall into heavy breathing over a novel. Warner's book is harmless—too fastidious and constipated to produce a fanatical response in any reader who is not already gripped by hysteria. The point rather is to see, in an act of clinical observation, that the rhetorical apparatus of the novel does have a political character. Insofar as the novel attains a residual effect at all, that effect is not attained through a process that respects the reader's autonomy. The process moves toward obliterating the reader's personal history, and with it the reader's volition. In that condition of anonymity and passivity, the reader escapes the burdens of consciousness, but the reader is also unresistant to the message that the process inscribes.

The sentimental style is the epideictic of fascism. Just as a ceremonial speech, for example, will ordinarily rehearse communal verities that are beyond controversy, and thus exhibit forms of persuasion that are substantively desiccated, the sentimental style exhibits a totalitarian rhetorical procedure without the sustained coercive components and the elaborated ideology that would allow totalitarianism really to work. The sentimental style exercises us in passivity, in obedience, and in the surrender of ourselves. For those of us who are secure in our identity, sentimentality may be only a fugitive indulgence. But for those of us who must struggle for an independent self-esteem, the sentimental style is another rehearsal of our subservience.

I close with a self-correction. When I wrote of Daniel Webster in connection with the sentimental style, I offered the suspicion that the repressive character of the style had its roots in an incipiently guilty conscience, perhaps with slavery as the unacknowledged cause. This novel and others of similar vintage and character have convinced me that the yearning for absolute control exhibited in the sentimental style more probably is rooted in the evangelical religious beliefs that were regnant in nineteenth-century America.

Those beliefs, which are both explored and illustrated in *The Wide, Wide World* yield, among other things, one bit of commanding advice that John gives the submissive Ellen near the end of the book. That advice, which is the closest this book ever gets to a paradox, I quote in full: "Read no novels." If everything called a novel were as psychologically despotic as this one, that advice could be received by us all with tears of welcome.

6
Ideological Justifications

On Wednesday, 13 July 1977, there was an extensive outage of electrical power in New York City. During the blackout, in certain parts of the city mobs of people broke into stores and carried away their contents. Acts of arson were committed. And television cameras photographed these activities for showing on subsequent news broadcasts. On Sunday, 17 July 1977, the text with which we are concerned appeared as an editorial in the *New York Times*.[1]

A BLIND NIGHT
Let a Nation Heed the "Animals"

Distance and perspective on the New York blackout leave ugly pictures in the mind. Smoke hovering over Brooklyn; shards of glass and leftover litter covering Pitkin Avenue. The anguished face of a merchant whose life's work and savings have just disappeared through a broken storefront. There are lithe, dark, young bodies darting past, laden with booty. There is a bearded black man, standing on a street of his own youth, surveying the scene and pronouncing the looters "rotten scum."

After the searing emotions experienced in those few hours of our communal life, it is important now to go back and to be quite clear about exactly what it was we saw. We surely saw losses that will diminish us for years to come; losses of business, of confidence, of faith, of racial civility, of neighborhood strength. We saw the loss of some portion of the reputation of our city. We saw the creation of ugly physical scars that may never heal.

But the darkness of Wednesday night made us see more about our city and our national policies than we have been able to see in a decade of sunshine. We were forced to confront what we as a nation have attempted to ignore ever since President Nixon assured us that it was all right to do so: that profound problems of race and poverty still lurk just beneath the surface of this fruitful society, that they pose a constant threat to a social fabric that is in fact surprisingly fragile.

Places called Bushwick, Brownsville, East Harlem and Williamsburg are miles beyond the ken of the thriving and thrusting Americans who make policy and mold opinions. The people who live in such places have always been beyond the vision of most Americans, but since the upheavals of the 60's, they have become even less visible. The new prominence of a relative handful of members of minority groups has, in the minds of the majorities in America, masked the enduring torments of poverty and race. But the invisibility of the inhabitants of the most forsaken, barren corners of urban America does not make their anguish or their rage less real. It simply makes their situation more hopeless, and they know it.

These people are victims of economic and social forces that they sense but do not understand: Puerto Ricans from an island where economic possibilities seem limited, and blacks from Southern farms where mechanization made them superfluous. Now, they are locked in a once-promising city, watching jobs and opportunity evaporate across the suburban horizon. Federal data indicate that the jobless rate for minority youth rose from 29 percent in 1973 to 33 percent in the recession of '73-

'74—and beyond 40 percent in the recovering economy of 1976. Small wonder that manpower specialists think minority youth unemployment is immune to upswings in the economic cycle.

In essence, the "animals" and the "scum" are people not bound to this society's values even by the semblance of equal opportunity in life. They have little reason to believe that the common good must maintain order and criminals must be punished swiftly and certainly. But if those are the only lessons that President Carter, Mayor Beame and the rest of us carry away from last week's anguish, we are in much worse trouble than we thought in the ugly hours before dawn on Thursday. In the blindness of that night, New York and America could see rage. We've been put on notice again. We may continue to ignore the terrible problems of poverty and race, but we must do so aware of the risks to both justice and peace.[2]

The very first sentence of the text insinuates the focus that the text will sustain. At the center of the perception that the text seeks to induce are "ugly pictures in the mind." The opening sentence is not, at first reading, remarkable. Only as the text is developed will we see that this early reference to "pictures in the mind" is the beginning of an orientation that the text assiduously cultivates, an orientation that is strikingly reflexive and introspective for an ostensibly political text.

Following that initial sentence, there are three brief visual images, and then the recapitulation of characters who had been imaged on television: the face of a merchant whose shop had been looted, a group of looters, and a witness to the looting.

The looters are "lithe, dark, young bodies," but the disapproving witness is a "bearded black man." Try this: "I was robbed (or raped or beaten) by a bearded black man"; or "I was robbed (or raped or beaten) by a lithe, dark, young body." The altered contexts establish the loading of the terms: the first formulation would probably be taken as a literal, descriptive statement, but the second formulation has to be interpreted as an irony. Moreover, a body is without responsibility, without will. Its character can only be its appearance. But a man is responsible, volitional, and his character is susceptible to moral judgment. Thus, the looters, by being bodies, are susceptible only to aesthetic or instrumental judgment, and by being lithe, dark, and young, to favorable aesthetic or instrumental judgment. But the disapproving witness, by being a man, must be held responsible for "pronouncing the looters 'rotten scum.' "

We are, then, presented in the introductory paragraph of the editorial with a distinction between aesthetically admirable, perhaps even sexually desirable, objects who are immune to moral judgment, and a man who pronounces a moral judgment. And the burden of the remainder of the editorial is to undermine the moral judgment that the man pronounces; thus leaving the lithe, dark, young bodies at the foreground of our perception of the event.

"After the searing emotions experienced in those few hours of our communal life, it is important now to go back and to be quite clear about exactly what it was we saw." The issue, then, is epistemological, not moral—a matter not of judging, but of perspective, of diagnosis. The referential event is "searing emotions experienced"—not lootings, not burnings, not riots, not actions of any kind, not the behavior of moral agents. And after the experiencing of emotions, "it is important now to go back and to be quite clear about exactly what it was we saw." The emotions are to be recollected in tranquility; they are to precede a quest for clarity and accuracy in their accompanying perceptions. What is important is the alignment of moral emotions with an objective correlative. And behind the quest for this alignment is a concession of the possibility of misalignment—the possibility that emotions may be detached from or ill-proportioned to a grounding in reality. The inquiry "what . . . we saw" is announced as important, but it is not warranted, perhaps out of a conviction that illicit emotions are sufficiently commonplace that no warranting is needed for an inquiry into the legitimacy of an emotion.

Note the passive construction of the sentence: "the searing emotions [that who?] experienced . . . it is important now [for who?] to go back. . . ." It is clear enough in the phrases *"our* communal life" and "what it was *we* saw" that some first-person plural is being addressed, but addressed more archly, more discreetly, more evasively than the grammatical structure of the sentence requires. Why? One can only answer in terms of function: the reference to an experience without a specification of the subject who does the experiencing joins the "pictures in the mind" of the initial sentence to sustain a focus on subjective states rather than objective events. Moreover, the absence of an articulate subject creates a condition of vagueness, so that it becomes easy for the text later to focus its readers on the emotions experienced by the looters (anguish and rage), and to allow consideration of "our" emotions to disappear from the text. Finally, there may be tact at work here. To suggest, at this early point, that only "we" experienced searing emotions, but that "they" (the looters) did not could have an overtone of invidious discrimination, especially to readers sensitive to nuances of ideological purity. Yet, the text addresses "us," not "them," and so it leaves the subject of experience vague until it can develop its control over our responses and bring us later to being attentive to "their" emotions and suppressing our own.

There follows for the remainder of the second paragraph of the text an inventory of what "we saw." What we saw were not actions but the effects of actions. We saw losses—the losses of material and moral goods. But does one *see* a loss? Not literally. Literally one experiences a loss. And so the verb "saw" here has to be taken as a synecdoche for "experienced," and the focus of our attention remains on our subjective state. The text continues into its second paragraph to contain our perceptions, to turn them inward, and to place the disorders of 13 July on their periphery. The subject of the text is emerging as "our reactions."

After the list of what we saw (experienced), the paragraph comes to an abstraction ("the reputation of our city") and finally to a literally visualizable object ("ugly physical scars"). Note that last item: "We saw the creation of ugly physical scars." We saw a "creation." The term is ordinarily eulogistic, and its context here is shaped into a curious passivity. Just as the sentence that opens this paragraph has an experience without an experiencer, so the sentence that concludes the paragraph has a creation without a creator. And what has been created? Scars. Symptoms of past injuries. Not wounds, but their aftermath. The injury is put behind us when we call it a scar. One senses here a certain hastening of history.

What is it, then, that we are to accept as what we saw? First, a series of our experiences. Then an abstraction. Finally, a potentially chronic residue of past affliction. No act. No actor. No motive.

Let me defer briefly an examination of the first sentence of paragraph three, and focus instead on the second: "We were forced to confront what we . . . have attempted to ignore since President Nixon assured us that it was all right to do so." The looting, then, performed a service. It compelled us to engage a truth that we had been refusing—refusing because of the influence of one of the most mendacious politicians of our time. The looting served a beneficent end. It edified us. It dispelled a willed mystery, an epistemological hypocrisy. (It seems a peculiarly modern phenomenon—one closely associated with political liberalism—that the refusal or even the disinclination to confront an unpleasant fact should occasion shame and, concomitantly, that the willingness to confront an unpleasant fact should occasion self-congratulations. There is a puritanical quality to this part of the liberal credo—an abjuring of aesthetic serenity in favor of an austere duty. From wearing hairshirts to taking cold baths to facing facts, a single generic form is being perpetuated.)

The remainder of the third paragraph lists the truths that we were brought to confront, and they are a series of cliches and mixed metaphors: problems lurk beneath the surface of a fruitful society threatening a fabric that is fragile. A coherent metaphor in this crucial place would, I think, have greatly empowered this text. Why is this initial statement of the peripeteia in so disintegrated a condition? One cannot be certain of the reasons without greater access to the mind of the rhetor than this text provides, but I shall speculate that the rhetor's attention and energy and skill are consumed with the task of transmuting an event intensely antipathetic to his political convictions into a historic memory that is, at its worst, politically neutralized and that may, at its best, actually serve his ideology. The details of the exposé that he is reporting may therefore be much less engaging to him than his imposition onto our perspective of the *form* of an exposé—teasing out the hidden moral that pervades the event. That the event conceals an ironic truth is more important to the rhetor than what that truth is. Faced with describing that truth, the rhetor's mind falls into cliches; he summons up the hoary remnants of stock phrases. A political ideology and its associated attitudes are stable in his mind; the disordered event and his audience's relationship to it are formless and kinetic. He wants to assimilate the latter to the former. And so it is understandable that the rhetor's artistry is invested in the work of that assimilation, and that his mind would repose into flaccidity when it occupies itself with its own anchoring.

Let us not leave the third paragraph without noting its opening sentence: "But the darkness of Wednesday night made us see more about our city and our national politics than we have been able to see in a decade of sunshine." The sentence is not without elegance. The reference to the darkness of the night is literal, but is transmuted into metaphor by the reversal of "darkness" into "sunshine" and the expansion of "night" into "decade." Another source of small delight in the sentence is the paradox of our being able to see more in the darkness than in the sunshine. The sentence is a concentration of coherent subtleties; it leaves the impression of a miniature eloquence. Only one tiny matter remains to arrest one's surrender to the charm of the sentence, and it is the phrase, "a decade of sunshine."

There are at least two ways of taking "a decade of sunshine." One way is fairly pedestrian for so soaring a sentence: "a decade of sunshine" may be taken to refer simply to the period between major power failures in New York City. There had been a power failure in 1965, but rather than having issued in civil disorder, that earlier power failure yielded an exuberant cohesiveness, a sense of common challenge and shared adventure, among the people who were affected. Alternatively, "a decade of sunshine" may be taken to refer to the ten-year period ending in 1977 as a sunny period in our civic and national life. Those two interpretations are perfectly compatible with one another, but if the latter interpretation is at all admissable, then the phrase "a decade of sunshine" may inadvertently illuminate some political values of the rhetor in the quickly transient way that a bolt of lightning illuminates a dark prospect. The decade 1967–77 was a time of turmoil on our campuses and in the streets of our cities. Think of the place-names of that decade: Birmingham, Watts, Detroit, Chicago, Morningside Heights, Altamont, Kent State. Think of the Days of Rage—indeed, the months and the years of it. How striking if that convulsive time should be called "a decade of sunshine." The clause in the sentence is not conditional; it is not "we would have been able to see." No, some real decade appears to be the referent, and the phrase therefore may be one of those inadvertent revelations of attitude so common to our discourse.

Sometimes the language tears the truth from our lips even when we think we don't know it, or know it, but intend not to say it. Sometimes the language forces ignorance to testify and concealment to disclose. There is a level at which our language is incorruptible. Even fashioned into lies, it can display a truth that betrays them. So may it be here with the phrase "a decade of sunshine" and the rhetor who wrote it. I do not mean to suggest that he has tried to lie to us, but rather that he may have succeeded in lying to himself. For if indeed this brief phrase betrays an attitude—if indeed that decade of popular frenzy is associated in the mind of this rhetor with the warmth and light of the sun, then maybe acts of civil disorder are not quite so deplorable to this rhetor as we may assume or as he himself may believe. Such acts instantiate social tensions and thus, through the acts, we come to know the tensions. Maybe this rhetor regards that knowledge, together with the moral emotions attendant on that knowledge, as valuable enough to justify the acts. It would be a calculation that one could endorse only with great circumspection on the editorial page of the *New York Times*. But it would be a calculation that would bring one to deflect attention from acts of civil disorder toward the diagnoses that such acts may recommend to us. It would be a calculation that would induce one to treat a tumult as if it were a text—to read it for its meanings, as this editorial does. And it would be a calculation that might bring one to view ten years of upheaval as "a decade of sunshine."

In the fourth paragraph the visional imagery is sustained. Visibility, obscurity, and invisibility are the conditions to which the subjects are referred. Or rather, the objects—for it is our perception, our seeing, that remains the subject of this argument, and the people in four designated places are the objects of that seeing. The looters, who were "lithe, dark, young bodies darting past"—an image charged with energy—have dissolved into the class of "people who live in such places"—"beyond the ken of the thriving and thrusting Americans who make policy and mold opinions." They are now "inhabitants of the most forsaken, barren corners of urban America"—passive, acted upon, ready at last to receive in the first sentence of paragraph five the appellation that will confirm their moral transmutation: "victims."

It is Lear who cries, "I am a man more sinned against than sinning." We see him in the play, at first a magisterial sovereign dispensing his powers, and then progressively a weakening old man who becomes a pitiable victim. The curve of tragedy transcribes a similarly lowering arc in this scenario, whose cumulatively disclosed theme is that the looters are people more sinned against than sinning: "These people are victims of economic and social forces that they sense but do not understand."

That sentence is the thesis on which the editorial pivots. By being "victims," "these people" solicit our sympathy. By sensing the forces that victimize them, "these people" can generate the moral emotions of anguish and rage and implicitly sanction their abreaction of those emotions under a principle of equity. But by not understanding the origins of their emotions, they are not responsible for them or their consequences. They have gained immunity from censure while retaining the prerogatives of volition. The condition is godlike, but it is premised on a reversal of conventional form. While we are familiar—most vividly in the painterly genre of the pietà—with the god who has become a victim, this text develops the victim into the moral equivalent of a god.

At this point in the text its major maneuvers have been

completed. The "animals" and "rotten scum" have undergone apotheosis, and what at the beginning was linked with a literally subhuman designation now has achieved a virtually superhuman ethos. What remains in the final two paragraphs is a fairly conventional argument for liberal policies. It is the four paragraphs of transition that fascinate—the reshaping of an emotional reaction so that it is virtually reversed: anger directed toward looters becomes shame for oneself and sympathy for them. Where in the second paragraph we, presumably, experienced "searing emotions" whose legitimacy depended on an objective correlative, now "their" sense that certain forces victimize them legitimates their anguish and rage. The issue that is sustained through the four paragraphs is the legitimacy of feelings—our unnamed but acute emotional reaction to the events of 13 July, and the looters' anguish and rage expressed in the events of 13 July. But a curious and interesting reversal has occurred. Whereas in Eliot's classic formulation of the objective correlative, an event or situation proportional to the feelings expressed by a moral agent had to exist in order to warrant those feelings, here we are approaching a view in which the feelings expressed by moral agents warrant a belief in the existence of an event or situation proportional to those feelings.

Beginning with rage and anguish, we then are invited to discern the conditions that legitimate them. To accept this pattern is to accept the implicit claim of this text that the looters were actuated by justiciary and socioeconomic considerations—considerations that they sensed but did not understand (thus disposing of a potential evidentiary problem). To reject this pattern would be to preserve the possibility of ascribing lower motives to the looters: greed, perhaps, or destructive malice. But we are not presented here with an explicated choice. Rather, while "we" are seared by emotions for which we are responsible, and which we are obliged to control and adapt to the objective conditions that constitute their rational provocation, the emotions of the "victims"—their anguish and rage—are the evidence that their objective conditions are deplorable. Both the rationality and the proportioning of their emotions are assumed to be appropriate.

We encounter, in this text, then, a manipulation of feeling-states in order to modify perceptions. And we end with a philosophically stunning possibility, adumbrated with such subtlety that we can almost believe it without acknowledging it. That possibility is that there is a class of human beings, called here "victims," whose emotions can verify propositions about reality. Not their intuitions, mind you; their emotions. One must suspect that there is something of the Noble Savage about this concept, that the ghost of Rousseau haunts these premises and, perhaps, other premises as well where a particular variety of liberal apologetics is being rehearsed.

This text also suggests that reflexivity and introspection may mark the discourse of liberal politics to a greater degree than we commonly note. I believe that a broader inquiry, but a microscopic one, into the texture of liberal discourse would reveal that the condition of our present text is typical and illustrative. Much liberal discourse is really less political than it appears. It is epistemological and inward-turning. It coaxes its auditors into self-concern and it sponsors, in the political sphere, a sacrificial egoism.

What may be less surprising is that the intense introspection that becomes, in the present text, a vehicle of political motive accumulates a detritus of shame. It is interesting that an origin of liberal guilt may be in the rhetorical strategies that liberalism hides from itself.

This analysis, focusing as it does on the latent content and inadvertent revelations of a text, shares some of the presuppositions of the text that it analyzes. The analysis too is liberal, at least to the limited degree to which liberalism can be associated with the public disclosure of motives and is, thus, a hermeneutical program. Indeed, this analysis may be characteristically liberal also in coming finally to turn upon itself and to achieve its present condition of reflexivity. But it must, before it concludes, seek to be liberal as well in the more general sense of sympathetic and compassionate, for justice demands an acknowledgment of the pressures under which this editorialist worked and of the wholly commendable values whose realization he sought.

The life of New York City could easily have been corroded

by racial enmity, even by retributive violence, in the days following 13 July 1977. There are always at least two problems attendant on civil disorder. One is the injury and destruction wrought by the disorder itself; the other is the emotional rancidness of its aftermath: the hatred that it expresses and the hatred that it creates. This editorial tried to inhibit the latter by highlighting the former. It undertook to ameliorate an effect by dwelling on a cause. It engaged the social afflictions that the disorder yielded by concentrating on the social afflictions that yielded the disorder.

It is only fair to note that those highly honorable intentions too are embedded in this text. The exposure of one's equivocations and contradictions is an embarrassment that can accompany even benevolent action, for only the imperfect seek the good.

7
Dramatic Form in Rhetorical Transactions

The simplest possible distinction between dramatic and narrative form is between showing and telling. If we view these two forms from the aspect of the audience, we can say that the audience of narrative is conscious of a mediator—the teller of the tale—who lives in a time of the narrator's own, and who recounts for the audience events that have occurred at a time other than the narrator's. In dramatic form, on the other hand, events are displayed without a mediator, and are apprehended by the audience as having a duration simultaneous with their apprehensions of them, and in a time to which the audience is imaginatively transported.

There are, then, two principal differences between narration and drama: Narration entails a narrator intervening between the action and auditor, while drama entails no mediation between the two. And narration entails three temporal referents—the action's, the narrator's, and the audience's—while drama entails no necessary temporal disparity between action and audience and, of course, no narrator at all.[1] There is a third important difference, and it has to do with the scope of the two forms, but that is a topic that I will defer for exploration later in this essay.

These distinctions between drama and narrative, although

confidently issued, can actually be quite blurred in specific cases. There are occasions, for example, when an ostensible narrative becomes a functional drama. Richard Nixon characterized his nationally televised speech of 3 November 1969—the Silent Majority speech—as "both a milestone and a turning point for my administration." It achieved a success beyond his most ardent hopes.[2] The speech was situated on the very boundary between narrative and drama. Although it virtually announced itself as a narrative of efforts to negotiate with North Vietnam, the speech was also strangely—but for Nixon, characteristically—reflexive for a deliberative address. It repeatedly coaxed the auditor to view the rhetor as its subject, and it thus cast the auditor into a relationship with the discourse that we ordinarily associate with epideictic occasions.

Early in the speech, after reciting the lamentable details of "the situation I found when I was inaugurated on January 20," Nixon reported that "there were some who urged that I end the war at once by ordering the immediate withdrawal of all American forces." But this usually self-repressed rhetor was always forthright about the wicked temptations that whispered their blandishments into his ear. Indeed, in his candor about forgone enticements, he even confessed to a sedulous calculation of the prospective advantages of wickedness.

> From a political standpoint this would have been a popular and easy course to follow. After all, we became involved in the war while my predecessor was in office. I could blame the defeat which would be the result of my action on him and come out as the peacemaker. Some put it to me quite bluntly: This was the only way to avoid allowing Johnson's war to become Nixon's war.

Naturally, as Nixon was wont to report, he spurned temptation and embraced virtue. But already in this speech, the focus was on the speaker, and the subject of the Vietnam War was being filtered through his presentation of himself.[3]

The speech did contain a narration of events, but it shaded

off into drama again in soliciting, finally, trust in the narrator, whose struggle and moral authority were advanced as its central issues. Its lengthy conclusion was replete with self references, with the rhetor situating himself—his hopes, his griefs, his aspirations, his popularity, his sense of his own duties—as the vehicle for national policy. From the body of the speech to its conclusion, the auditor was first being told and then being shown: told of diplomatic exchanges and negotiations, then shown the representation of a dedicated leader in whom the auditor was to have faith.

Even the narrative passages of the speech were so shaped that they ended by focusing on the narrator. For example, after an early recitation of arguments against "precipitate withdrawal of American forces from Vietnam," the conclusion: "For these reasons, I rejected the recommendation that I should end the war by immediately withdrawing all of our forces. I chose instead to change American policy on both the negotiating front and battlefront." The policy was enunciated as a choice of the speaker, who made himself the subject of the sentences.

The most extended narrative section of the speech—a recounting of efforts to negotiate a settlement—was introduced with some fanfare about secrecy and disclosure, which had been a Nixon theme since the Hiss case: "Tonight I am taking the unprecedented step of disclosing to you some of our other initiatives for peace—initiatives we undertook privately and secretly because we thought we thereby might open a door which publicly would be closed." Nixon the Candid, who had revealed the secrets of Hiss's treason and, in his Checkers speech, the secrets of his own finances, now revealed the secrets of his attempts to end the war. Nixon was, in this address, not the medium through whom a tale was transmitted. Rather, the tale was the medium for the transmission of its teller's moral portrait.

Nixon's shift of focus from Vietnam to himself, whether calculated or instinctive, was a shrewd maneuver. It brought attention away from a bankrupt policy to a still prestigious presidency. By reinforcing himself as an object of trust and deference, he was better able to manipulate events without having to risk public justifications of the manipulation. By not having defended a policy specific enough to bind him, he was left able to do anything that seemed to comport with his self-representations, which afforded him very great latitude.

Our distinction between narrative and drama brings us to comprehend Nixon's discussions of Vietnam policy and of his vision of America as incidental to another theme. The central concern of this speech was his lifelong preoccupation: his power. That theme united the subject of Nixon's confrontation with Ho Chi Minh—his rival for power in Vietnam—with the subject of his confrontation with the antiwar movement—his rivals for power in the United States. Nixon's speech—a slab of narrative sandwiched between two passages of self-dramatization—projected himself as the sole alternative to those two loci of rivalry. The rage and indignation that the speech inspired in anti-Nixon critics is a measure of the extent to which he had trapped even them within the terms of his scenario. In a pattern that he repeated throughout his career, Nixon, through dramatic form, had made himself the major issue.

Characteristically, the very imperfection of Nixon's acting in the role in which he cast himself heightened the auditors' awareness that Nixon was playing a public role, and that it was distinguishable from his private persona. The maladroitness with which Nixon represented himself made the public-private distinction salient whenever he spoke. His chronic awkwardness, the zeal of his reassurances about his own motives, the excess—in both quantity and cunning—of the allusions to himself: all contributed to the visibility of Nixon's self-creation, and hence to his becoming the subject of any issue he addressed. This speech was typical of him.

Nixon laminated both sides of his narration of Vietnam policy with a dramatic soliloquy, played against two offstage voices, one from Hanoi and the other from the streets, and he projected his own voice as the only one of the three that spoke both English and patriotism. Those three voices, uneven in their volume, were sounded to the Silent Majority—that mute public which Nixon's speech helped to create by its very articulation of them.

Insofar as Nixon purported to act as the prolocutor for the voiceless, focusing attention explicitly on the feelings that he felt on their behalf, he was inviting auditors to apprehend him as a performer and to appreciate his art. His was an inventive art. He was inventing a president.

In the middle, narrative section of the speech, the number of first-person references diminished, only to increase again in the long peroration. Nixon's speech serially deployed drama, then narration, and then drama again.

There have also been literary experiments—some of them successful—that have sought to fuse narrative and dramatic forms in one way or another. For example, Thornton Wilder's *Our Town* has a narrator on the stage who, at crucial moments during the play, intervenes as a mediator of the dramatic events, sets the stage, provides interpretation for the audience, and reinforces the temporal plurality that we associate with narrative by emphasizing in the audience's "present" the "pastness" of the play's episodes and characters. Such achievements as *Our Town*, however, do not compromise the fundamental distinction between dramatic and narrative forms. They represent experiments in the amalgamation of the forms; that they characteristically combine these forms by sequential rather than simultaneous presentation of them serves as further warrant for the distinction itself.

The passage in Lyndon Johnson's voting rights speech of 1965 in which Johnson talked of his own ambitions as president intrudes a dramatic form into a narrative account. That is, the passage is a representation of character, so drawn as to seek the admiration of the audience. The audience was solicited to observe the virtues of the rhetor even as he addressed them. This passage of fetid self-display is evidence that there is nothing inherently superior about dramatic form as a rhetorical medium, but it also illustrates that the rhetorical differences between narrative and dramatic forms pivot on their effects.

Narrative (telling) becomes drama (showing) at the point at which the credibility of the narrator becomes a salient issue to the auditor. To the extent that the narrator's credibility is assumed—to the extent that the auditor relies comfortably on

the narrator as a reliable conduit of truth—the auditor apprehends the form as narrative. To the extent that the narrator's
credibility is salient—to the extent that, for whatever reason,
the auditor is brought to doubt or to reserve trust in the narrator, or even to become conscious of the narrator's intervention as an intrusive element of the audition—the auditor experiences the form as dramatic. It is dramatic because the
object of the auditor's judgment has become the narrator, and
that object is not being reported; it is being directly observed.

Any narrative presents the credibility of the narrator as an
issue, but not always to the same degree.[4] Two factors influence this credibility: the narrator's ethos and the narrator's
presence. Both of these factors can be manipulated, within
limits. To the degree that the narrator's presence is compressed, the capacity of that narrator's credibility to be manipulated is also compressed. The more evident the narrator, the
more evidence about the narrator can be introduced.

For example, in the cases of both scientific and journalistic
reportage, a formulary pattern typically dominates the narration of material, and that pattern minimizes the presence of
the narrator, sometimes to the point of effacement. In the case
of scientific reportage, the pattern, which is strictly enforced
by professional journals in a standardized *dispositio,* consists
of detached presentation of experimental procedures and of
findings, extensively in passive voice and with no overt ten-
dentiousness allowed. In the case of journalistic reportage,
the famous pyramidal structure is employed to convey what
purports to be an objective account of an event. In both cases,
the individuality and character of the narrator—indeed, the
auditor's very consciousness of the narrator's presence—is
suppressed by the conventions of the genre. Consequently,
the generic conventions work to diminish the credibility of
the narrator as an issue in the transaction between the message and its auditor.

By contrast, the exile's account of terror and repression in
El Salvador or Ethiopia or Cuba—presented not by a passive
observer of events but rather by an active participant in
them—presents more prominently an issue of credibility.

Such testimonial narrative will affect auditors only to the extent that they credit the narrator. The narrative component of the transaction is therefore impure, for the exhibition of the putative narrator is as important as the narration itself. "I am the man, I suffer'd, I was there" is, by the definition controlling the present inquiry, drama, not narrative.

In the case of dramatic form, there is no issue of the credibility of the narrator because there is no narrator. But because dramatic form is involved in the unmediated observation of actions, the auditor's own epistemic competence can be made an issue in drama. *Roshomon* and *Six Characters in Search of an Author* are examples of dramas that challenge the ability of the auditor to apprehend the truth among the conflicting possibilities that the drama presents. There is, however, no corresponding rhetorical genre in which the perception of the auditor is brought into question. Typically in rhetorical transactions, the perception of the auditor is not undermined; on the contrary, it is given confidence by the presentation.

Admittedly, there is a well-documented procedure of persuasion, sometimes called brainwashing, by which an auditor, who is usually enduring physical restraint and induced exhaustion, is brought to a condition of extreme self-doubt, but this condition of individuated anomie is preliminary to radical conversion—to the generation of new beliefs and the realignment of basic commitments.[5] And throughout such a process, the authority of the rhetor and the capacity of the rhetor's language to convey truth are sustained unchallenged.

Rhetorical discourses seldom seek to generate doubts about themselves. The only doubt they ordinarily promote is directed at their antitheses. Most rhetorical discourses can be interpreted as seeking to regulate an audience's conception of a subject and its definition of the issues attending that subject. Even Emerson, whose deepest convictions made him diffident about exercising influence, contrived to persuade his audiences that they should seek a condition of convictional autonomy.[6]

The credibility of the source, then, is an issue attending

narrative that cannot attend drama in the same way. We may doubt that events we directly observe are representative or significant or authentic, but such doubts lead to the discrediting of a body of evidence, not—as in narrative—a source of evidence. In drama, to discredit a source of evidence would be to discredit our own perception. In drama, we know no more than we observe.

Showing engages the auditor differently from telling. In dramatic form, the auditor observes actions that elicit judgment. The variety of options for judgment that drama may create for the auditor is virtually incalculable, ranging from melodrama, which elicits the unambiguous, narrowly focused judgments associated with the sentimental style, to a presentation in which ambiguities and irresolutions are multiplied into the infinity of a hall of mirrors.

In the telling of something, by contrast, the interpretations of the teller come between the tale and the auditor. The intrusiveness of those interpretations are variable. The auditor's freedom to form judgments of narrated events is expanded in proportion to the simplicity of the report. To the extent that the narrator appears to be a neutral conduit, relaying in grammatically simple, declarative sentences the narrator's uninterpreted observations, the auditor is left relatively free to construct a response. But more complex or embellished narrative—narrative that displays the distinctive marks of the narrator—can achieve the auditor's freedom of interpretation only at the expense of the narrator's credibility. At the point at which the narrator's credibility becomes a principal issue, narrative would have crossed the boundary into drama.

One can imagine a narrative in which the narrator is genuinely confused or afflicted with doubt or lacking confidence in his perceptions. It would be a tale told by a skeptic. To the extent that a narrator was in this condition, the narrator's frame of mind would be the focus of the narrative and the events unreliably reported by the narrator would be mere vehicles for illuminating that frame of mind. That result too would be closer to drama than to narrative as conventionally understood. That is, it would be a showing more than a telling.

The narrator may express doubt about something in the narration, but when that happens, the doubt is shared by the audience; it would be a doubt about the same subject, not about the narrator. Doubt of the narrator shades off into drama insofar as it foregrounds the narrator's capacity to perceive and understand. One may believe a narrator, observing his testimony, testing his account against one's experience and against alternative accounts, or one may mistrust a narrator. At some point during the course of acquiring mistrust of the narrator, the weight of the auditor's perception shifts from apprehending the narrator as a conduit of a subject to apprehending the narrator as, himself, the subject. In the latter condition, the narrator would have become detached from the narration, and the narration would have become an instrument not in the disclosure of its ostensible subject, but in the disclosure of the narrator's reliability and credibility. The latter condition is dramatic, in the sense that the auditor would be making judgments prompted by unmediated observations that warranted those judgments; the auditor would be responding with immediacy to the revelations of character. A true narration would have its subject, not its agent, at the center of the auditor's attention, and would have a judgment of the past as the issue of that focus.

Narration—as the term is being construed here—has a more limited expressive range than drama. Narration requires that the attention of its auditor be more focused, more regulated, more temporally constrained: a condition that has not always obtained throughout human history, but that does seem to obtain now.[7]

If, with the distinction between dramatic form and narrative form—between showing and telling—we turn to the three Aristotelian genres of rhetorical discourse, we can find elements of order and system. It is evident, for example, that the genre of forensic discourse must be, by its nature, closely tied to narrative form. The audience of forensic discourse sits in judgment of the past, and the contending rhetors intervene between that audience and the events they are to judge. The audience apprehends the forensic rhetor as a mediator advocating, in a time simultaneous with their own, an interpretation of an action that has been completed so that it can now be judged.

When we observe a criminal trial as spectators, we may be fascinated by what we would call the "drama" of the proceeding. And indeed, we would be confronting recollections and recountings of past events disclosed within a juridical structure that, because it is adversarial and because it culminates in resolution, is dramatic in its immediacy. The observation of a trial can be an experience as consuming and suspenseful as any drama, but many of the discrete discourses of its participants are narratives. Narratives are elicited by the lawyers from witnesses, and narratives are likely to constitute the summations by the lawyers: narratives of the trial itself. The observer of a trial, then, witnesses a drama suffused with narratives, a drama that is recapitulated in mutually incompatible narratives near its end.

It is important to note, especially in accounting for the place of narrative in the forensic genre, that narrative occurs in rhetorical discourses but that drama occurs in rhetorical transactions. The medium of narrative is language. But the medium of drama is the mise-en-scène: the whole of the rhetorical transaction, including not only the linguistic, but also the scenic, the choric, and the mimic. Anything within the drama may directly signify: the gesture, the facial expression, even the inert object; but the narrative is only words. It is, then, only in the words of the forensic genre that narrative appears.

The genre of epideictic, on the other hand, is more closely tied to dramatic than to narrative form, even in its words. In Aristotle's account, the audience of epideictic is focused on "the force and merit of the speech." The manifest content of an epideictic discourse may be the past or future, but its latent content is always the present as it implicitly beckons the audience to render a judgment of the rhetor's skill and virtuosity. The epideictic rhetor shows and even his telling is a showing.

Deliberative discourse is the intermediate genre, exhibiting at varying historical moments sometimes narrative and at other times dramatic capacities. We read now, with awe and

wonder, some of the deliberative masterpieces of the past—
Burke's "Speech on Conciliation" or Webster's "Reply to
Hayne"—and we are reminded of the shrunken narrative
powers of our own age. We do not now have orators who can
create scenes of such magnitude, who can project an argument that is imaged in the enterprises of a vast, teeming, vi-
brant polity, endowed with a history and populated with the
complex contentions of diverse interests.

Nor have we audiences who have cultivated the capacity to
assimilate such encyclopedic narratives. The dominance of
deliberative discourse by narrative form is a part of our past,
but a part that is increasingly remote and probably irretrieva-
ble. It has yielded to the dominion of dramatic form, and that
dominion is at once a symptom and a cause of other, more
generalized and significant tendencies in our civic lives.

It is, of course, television that most conspicuously exhibits
this dominance of deliberative discourse by dramatic form.
Television has caused our political judgments to be formed
with increasing frequency by what we experience as a direct
observation of events rather than by the narration of events
in consecutive discourse. The Aristotelian formulation would
be: Television has enhanced the importance of ostensibly in-
artistic proofs, and has concomitantly reduced the importance of ostensibly artistic proofs.

The dispensation of the Aristotelian tradition is to see
drama as an imitation, a mimesis; not a report or recounting
of an event; rather a simulacrum, a facsimile of one. But one
of the technical accomplishments of our symbol-ridden age is
the ability to erase the shadow between the event and its representation, to contrive the elements of drama in such a way
that performance and action are one. And audiences, in the
conviction that they are perceiving unmediated realities,
form their commitments through rational inferences about
what they have observed rather than what they have been
told.

Moreover, our intellectual life is pervaded by the metaphor
of drama as an explanatory principle. From the Oedipal
theory of Sigmund Freud to the role theory of Erving Goff-
man, from the dramatistic pentad of Kenneth Burke to the

ethnomethodology of Clifford Geertz, this past century's systematic thought about human behavior has been deeply influenced, in vocabulary and perspective, by the metaphor of drama.

The metaphor is continuously nourished by the media, most notably by television reportage, which emphasizes the dramatic qualities of subjects and abjures subjects that are dramatically deficient.

Consider as an example the once addictively fascinating controversy over Watergate. A large audience watched the summer-long hearings on television, hearings that established a cast of characters and a basic plot.

The audience was well prepared for senators Sam Ervin and Howard Baker. Twenty million childhoods spent with Batman and Robin, and a hundred television episodes of the wise old cop and the impetuous young cop had prepared them to receive and understand the avuncular joining of youth and age to form a heroic coupling. And before the senatorial committee and its national audience passed the procession of witnesses—the once powerful, now fallen—each contributing to that quest for truth that has actuated drama since Sophocles—that quest for the ultimate, hidden violator of our taboos who had to be found and purged from the polity before the collective curse could be lifted from us.

Against the adverse perspective on Watergate, strongly limned by the Senate hearings, we had the prime antagonist—the Fisher King himself—Richard Nixon, curiously paralyzed in the elaboration of his own defense, unable to scale it in sufficiently dramatic terms to rescue him.[8] Nixon's effort was to answer each new revelation with a discrete defense, and while the revelations grew organically into a cohesive plot in which Nixon finally was the conspirator and villain, his antithetical responses were dispersed and formless. He thus remained frantically defensive and ultimately implausible. The comprehensive form that Nixon lacked could have come only as a dramatic recasting of the Watergate episode—a reinterpretation of the same actions and characters within the governance of a different plot.

We have come to expect and to demand that the media

function dramatically, not alone with fictional material, but with the literal as well. And so, the dramatization of deliberative messages proceeds as an inevitable consequence.

When narrative was paramount, the object of serious rhetorical activity was to characterize the world in such a way that the rhetor and audience came to share common presuppositions. The spacious narratives of eighteenth- and nineteenth-century British and American oratory, for example, worked to adumbrate a universe of values into which the auditor was placed and with reference to which the auditor adjudicated the issue addressed by the oration. Dramatic form, by contrast, is much less likely to elaborate a context for the apprehensions of the auditor. With the rise of dramatic form in rhetorical situations, auditors are left with their private worlds intact, and are asked only to assent to a more particular construction of a local reality—asked to assent to it through their direct apprehension of it in the form of drama.[9] Naturally, the narrative approach to rhetorical activity made for more expansive and historically encompassing disquisitions, for whole polities had to be imaged in the discourse. Dramatic form accommodates a greatly abbreviated discourse, one focused on the particulars of the skit. It is a form better adapted than narrative to the attenuated attention span of modern audiences, and to our heightened awareness of the distinction between our public and our private lives.

A recurrent character of rhetorical argument is its logical fractionality. In the case of the enthymeme, which Aristotle defined as the "very body and substance of persuasion," only a part of its syllogistic structure is usually explicit. The minor premise is said aloud and subjected to demonstration. The major premise is not ordinarily explicated out of confidence that it is a conviction shared by rhetor and audience alike. For example, it is seldom in a criminal trial that the prosecutor will say, "Stealing is wrong," just as it is seldom that the defense attorney will say, "Innocent people should not be punished." Such statements are simply unnecessary. Both propositions are so unquestioningly believed by all who participate in a trial that their being said is superfluous. Instead of rehearsing what everyone already believes, the attorneys in a trial spend their time arguing propositions that are in contention: "The defendant is a thief," or "The defendant is innocent." Each attorney is confident that a juror, upon accepting a contested proposition, will combine it syllogistically with an appropriate major premise, and will draw therefrom a valid inference. The transcripts of trials can be understood only if one interprets these contested propositions as minor premises of syllogisms that are completed in the heads of the participants.

Similarly in the case of the example—the rhetorical version of inductive logic—the single case is persuasive only if it is interpreted by the audience as representative of a genre of such cases. If history is the source of inductive evidence, as it frequently is in deliberative situations—the familiar argument, for instance, that the consequences of placating Hitler in the Munich agreement argue for resistance to any expansionary regime—then the repertory of analogous situations is severely limited. An auditor must make portentous commitments on the basis of one or two examples. Notoriously, such decisions cannot satisfy the requirements of inductive logic, but the human condition is inescapably bound by the necessity of either making choices or loosing the power to choose, of acting or being acted on, of projecting ourselves into an unknowable future, and we are left with no logical options except the imperfect ones that we exercise.

The term "sign" is especially apposite in interpreting the place of rhetorical argument in narrative. The narrator supplies not full logical demonstrations, but rather the tokens of them. The narrator provides the partial display of an argumentative warrant that remains otherwise implicit, and the audience credits or discredits this demonstration—less a proof than an allusion to proof—on the basis of their general sense of its validity and of their attitude toward the rhetor. In narrative as in the dramatic skit, rhetorical procedure is distinguished by compression and abbreviation, by a telegraphy that reminds us what a remarkable proportion of rhetorical practice is tacit, implicatory, hidden.

Increasingly, the circumstance in which narrative form dominates deliberative discourse, to the virtual exclusion of dramatic form, is restricted to that in which the audience has accepted or is prepared to accept a single interpretation un-questioningly. Franklin Roosevelt's War Message—the speech before the joint session of Congress on 8 December 1941—is an example of narrative dominating a rhetorical transaction. In that brief, powerful speech, Roosevelt described, with a self-disciplined detachment, the series of military actions that Japan had taken the previous day. His narrative of events was preceded and followed by strong interpretations, but the narration itself was simple, unadorned, ostensibly objective. The speech was given to a country that was without any disposition to question the rhetor's interpretation of events. But that circumstance is hardly typical of a deliberative situation. The typical deliberative situation is rather one in which incompatible viewpoints are competing for the auditor's allegiance. In such a competition, the rhetors are presenting more than their narratives; they are also presenting themselves as competitors. Their fates may hinge as much on the latter effort as the former.

In 1934, Gertrude Stein gave four lectures on narrative at the University of Chicago. As one would expect, the lectures are not argued in any conventional fashion; yet, they are full of suggestive insights. Their conception of narrative is expansive: "Narrative is what anybody has to say in any way about anything that can happen has happened will happen in any way." [10] Nevertheless, as her definition makes clear, Stein was careful to preserve the conception of narrative as necessarily entailing a narrator.

In her singular way, Stein explored the influence of epistemic change on the function of narrative:

> When one used to think of narrative one meant a telling of what is happening in successive moments of its happening the quality of telling depending upon the conviction of the one telling that there was a distinct succession in happening that one thing happened after something else and since that happening in succession was a profound conviction in every one then really there was no difference whether any one began in the beginning or

the middle or the ending because since narrative was a progressive telling of things that were progressively happening it really did not make any difference where you were at what moment you were in your happening since the important part of telling anything was the conviction that anything that everything is progressively happening. But now we have changed all that we really have. We really now do not really know that anything is progressively happening and as knowledge is what you know and as now we do not know that anything is progressively happening where are we then in narrative writing and what has this to do with poetry and with prose if it has that is to say if poetry and prose have anything to do with anything and anything has anything to do with narrative that is telling of what is happening.[11]

Stein here is occupied with the literary fracturing of "progressive happening," with the dispersion of consecutive moments and with their expansion or contraction. These are techniques of manipulation for which television has a unique proficiency. Television can accelerate the moment or retard it, freeze it within a frame, subordinate it to a montage, all the while preserving the directness of our apprehension of it. Through that medium, we have been able to witness, again and again, the moment when Jack Ruby shot Lee Harvey Oswald in the stomach, the moment when Nixon waved good-bye to power from the door of a helicopter, the moment when the Iranian revolutionary guards displayed their captives from the American embassy, the moment when John Hinckley, Jr., fired at Ronald Reagan.

Each of these episodes, a narrative fragment but a complete dramatic skit, acquires the power of evocation. It is capable of summoning to active memory a congeries of events and the attitudes that were originally associated with them. These episodes, charged with mnemonic potency, are difficult to account for in traditional terms. They surely are not stories, although they have some of the same formative influences that some stories have; but they leave us, as Stein has observed of fragmented narrative, not really knowing "that anything is progressively happening."

Neither can these episodes be regarded as enthymematic premises: the presuppositions from which we derive our convictions. Their form is phenomenal rather than propositional. Yet, they come to be lodged at the core of memory as stubbornly as enthymematic premises, and they bear strongly on our beliefs about our collective experiences. These iconic episodes are electric with meaning for an audience to whom they are actions observed. And the observation of action is the essence of the dramatic experience.

Of course, we should expect an effort to exploit commercially the expressive compression of drama. Such efforts are abundant in the twenty-second dramas that constitute much of television advertising: the little skits in which the initially reluctant consumption of the cereal is rewarded by pleasure, or the pain is first suffered and then relieved by the ingestion of the medicine. Obviously, the creators of these episodes hope that they will have persuasive force, and the sponsors who pay for them are betting that they will. If these skits induce belief in the proposition that the product should be acquired, then they clearly are probative; they have to be regarded as specimens of rhetorical proof.

Although these commercial skits are full-blown, miniature dramas with beginnings, middles, and ends, they may come closer to a narrative function than the more prepossessing, literal enactments that mark our memories. Logically, these commercial skits function as minor premises in enthymemes. In order to credit these proffered minor premises—to make the skit probative—the auditor has to have some attitude of sympathy for or trust in the central character in the skit. The character is, in effect, giving testimony, even as a narrator does, and the religious tradition of bearing witness is subtly invoked in these pitches. What is important to our consideration of the persuasive uses of dramatic form is the effort in these commercial skits to abolish the intermediary—the salesperson, the pitchman, the narrator—the effort so to frame the testimony that it appears to be dramatic action, directly observed.

Paradoxically, television's capacity to saturate compressed episodes with meaning is complemented by an alternative capacity for protraction that can emotionally deplete an audience. The Vietnam War was on every evening news program for nearly ten years. It was a subject repeating itself until a public was surfeited, jaded, pressed beyond patience by the sheer, unrelenting reiteration. Later, the Watergate scandal was persistently presented for over two years until, as with Vietnam, a public longed for relief, less perhaps from the event than from the subject of the event.[12] Later still, the incessant reports about the American hostages in Iran—every evening for 444 evenings—became to Carter what the gadfly had been to Io.

Television has the ability to make an acute problem into a chronic problem, and that ability is peculiar to the medium. Newspapers can be read selectively, or not at all; radio can be ignored; but television's addictive quality—its capacity to embed the insufferable within the irresistible—gives it the power to persist even beyond the patience of its audience. It is the nag of media.

Moreover, its nagging sometimes tempts rhetors to imprudence. Nixon, baited beyond endurance by the daily news reports on Watergate, took to television himself with increasing frequency in an effort to compensate for his adverse publicity. His manic visibility ended by making him a nag and a bore, even as the subject of Watergate had become, and he ultimately suffered the dual disrepute of being both a scandal and a scandalmonger.

By shaping controversy to the form of drama, television imposes its own priorities and perspectives on political events. It leaves the actors with the option either of conforming to the medium or of being distorted by it. That may be why there has been a rough correlation between the acquisition of political power and the resentment of television. The resentment is expressed in bitter complaints about television from political figures who want to control the scenario of public debate. But the medium converts persons into dramatis personae, and they must play the roles into which the medium has cast them or retire entirely from the stage. Even the words that they utter—their own words—are subordinated to a configuration not of their making. We are confronting here not so much falsification as the intractability of form. And in the case of political leaders, the form exercises a tyranny over just those people who are most sensitive to power and most skilled at manipulating it.

The paradigm of this is the film *Roshomon*. The film is about a killing, a killing that we see enacted four times, each time through the eyes of a different witness. We see the killing from the point of view of the victim's wife, the killer, an unseen bystander, and finally—thanks to the intervention of a spiritualist—the victim himself. Each perspective on the killing implies its own judgments of character and culpability; each possesses its own moral priorities; each is possessed by its own interests.

What was the killing really like? The point of the drama, of course, is that the question is idle. We have no single narrative of the event, but instead, multiple narratives, each of which casts a different light on the credibility of all the narrators. We auditors are forced back upon our own constructions by a perspectival anarchy. This situation of rhetorical disorder, which television proliferates, denies to anyone the role of narrative authority, for in place of a voice telling a story it installs a dissonant chorus of contradictions.

The medium of television and the dramatic form that is its most attractive vehicle prohibit rhetors from speaking in the single voice that most of them would prefer. Hence we have heard from one public figure after another, reacting with despair at their own televised images, the same message that we heard from the Watergate-tormented Nixon ("I'm not a crook!"): *That is not really me. That luminous figure, that play of shadow and light—it is not really me.* We first heard it from Nixon in 1960, then from Goldwater in 1964, and later from Johnson and Humphrey and McGovern and Carter: *That is not the way I am; it is not really me. I am more nearly whole, better intentioned, more complex, more comprehending.*

But of course, any figure who is on television becomes thereby a public figure—even if, as Andy Warhol remarked, it is only for fifteen minutes—so that the medium prescribes its own distinctions between the public and private domains. This capacity of the medium for social regulation was vividly apparent in an astonishing documentary series first shown in

1973, "An American Family," and in the subsequent reactions of the subjects, the Loud family, especially Pat Loud, the mother.

The producers of "An American Family" filmed actual scenes of tension and interaction in a Los Angeles private home. The Loud family had consented to the presence of the camera within their household, doubtless in the conviction that pictures don't lie, and in the enviable confidence that the publication of their personal lives would not perturb them. But they suffered from complacency, if not hubris, in their naive trust that their appearances coincided with their experiences of themselves, and that they could therefore be indifferent to how they appeared. They had not anticipated what it would mean to them to have their personal lives become clinical data for a documentary, much less for their troubles to be publicly displayed.[13] And so, after the twelve-hour documentary had been shown on television to much acclaim, and after millions of viewers watched the relationships among a prosperous, handsome family suffer strain and then disintegration, the Louds themselves appeared on the Dick Cavett program and, with an intelligence and moral seriousness that the documentary had never hinted at their having, they expressed their indignation at the documentary's epistemic betrayal.

Tolstoy's famous observation about families suggests part of the explanation for the Loud's reaction: They were willing enough to have their happy typicality recorded, but their miserable singularity was another matter. Typicality is indeed a public matter; but singularity is private. These are issues of definition. And thus the language itself imposed a distinction on the Louds that they had been unwilling to make for themselves. Taken unexpectedly by misfortune, they wanted to suffer it outside the camera's range. Only martyrs choose to suffer in public, and martyrdom is not a popular cynosure among Southern Californians who own their own swimming pools.

That the Louds were *echt* Californian added further strain to the public-private distinction. Californians, especially Southern Californians, have, in an abundance disproportionate to the rest of the country, salubrious impulses toward wholeness. They experiment constantly with the construction of a social order in which the public and private realms are fused while, at the same time, individuality is preserved—a very difficult feat. Insouciant people can make this quest for personal integration look easier to attain than it is. The Louds seem to have thought that they had achieved an indivisible poise, until Pat Loud found that her relaxed tolerance did not extend to her husband's sleeping around. Her discovery of his infidelity produced a crisis in this attractive family, and that private crisis, which television made public, was succeeded by the public crisis, which pain made private, of their having allowed their misery to become an entertainment for strangers.

The moments of their lives selected for presentation were chosen on a basis different from their experience of their own living. They had not counted on the inevitable disparity between actor and observer. Expecting their own experience of themselves to be immortalized on film, they found instead what they regarded as a distorting selection of their behaviors chosen in obedience to requirements of plot and form, a selection that was alien to the ways that they had lived their moments. They looked, with outrage, on what they could only regard as a falsification. They knew the reality: they had lived it. They could no more deny the authenticity of their own experience than they could deny the authenticity of themselves, for the two were indistinguishable. Inevitably, the product of such representations is outrage.

The dramatization of their lives was an interpretation. It cast their raw experience into a grammar that rendered it amenable to judgment. But their lived experience was injudicable except with reference to its underlying rationality, its inevitability, its following inexorably from the vivid impulses and unutterable aspirations that constitute motives and that elude mechanical reproduction. Their relationship to television recapitulated that of politicians, who must face the Louds' dilemma as a chronic occupational hazard.

Martin Luther, in the most dramatic scene of his life, said, "Ich kann nicht anders." He spoke for us all. What, after all, could any of us have done otherwise? We act and we are acted on, sometimes with confidence, sometimes with fear, but having sought something that seemed at the time worthy of seeking, only our overtness was on display for the camera to record. The motives that to us redeemed our acts were invisible. Yet, we experienced those motives as a seamless part of the behavior that expressed them, and hence a record that registers only our conduct must seem to us a pathetic amputation. The visual chronicle is denied our explanation of ourselves, our trajectory toward the recorded deed, our sense of the preemptive rightness of our recollected actions.

The camera distorts us because we could have done no other. What did Luther end by saying? "Gott helfe mir!" Yes indeed. It could well be the prayer of any public figure in the television age.

There is a dual alienation that occurs in televised rhetorical transactions. The first is the alienation of which Pat Loud bitterly complained: the alienation of the public figure from her image. Its major symptom is the complaint from public figures that television misrepresents actions and distorts intentions, that the medium exacerbates the discrepancy between appearance and reality by its perverse exaltation of appearance.

The second alienation is bound up in the paradox that the very intrusiveness of television generates a residual distancing of the persona from the public. Television creates expectations of intimacy that it can seldom meet, so that the performer's hidden, private personality casts a shadow across the public persona, and what the person is "really like" becomes an active perplexity rather than remain a dormant mystery. The medium invites us to a condition of personal knowledge that the medium cannot satisfy.

In contrast to the adversities of other performers, Ronald Reagan was not disconcerted by television. His equanimity would have to be accounted for, in part, by his comfort with dramatic form: his ability to play a convincing role in historical events, to project the appropriate attitudes and emotions. Reagan did not publicly complain about television. His careful rationing of his televised appearances and the strict control over those appearances exercised by his staff suggest, at the very least, a cautious respect for the medium's potentialities. He appeared buoyant and confident in his engagement with the medium. There was no wariness in the performance, as had been divulged, for example, by Carter's nervous shuffle: a physical paroxysm that sometimes seized him during transitions in his speeches, and that simulated the anticipatory recoil of a boxer knowing that he is about to take a punch.

If Reagan had any unease about television, it was hidden, to be tentatively inferred from the relative scarcity of his appearances, their lack of spontaneity, and his more frequent reliance on radio, the medium most compatible with his line-reading abilities. But Reagan's theatrical skill was a rarity among national politicians. One would have to go back more than a quarter of a century before Reagan—to Kennedy—to find his equal in poise with the medium and its characteristic forms.[14]

Despite the inability of many public figures at once to create their own images and to conform to the dramatic demands of television, their loss of self-creation is not necessarily the public's loss as well. Dramatic form comports not only with television as a medium, but more generally with the kinds of understanding we are prepared to have of political experience. Although we may often be tempted to interpret the effects yielded by dramatic form as distortion or sensationalism, the dramatic shaping of controversial material is also a vehicle for organizing and understanding controversy. Dramatic form has the epistemological function of fixing human events into a condition that enables us to comprehend them.

The form accommodates the representation of conflicting interests, playing out their tensions in situations of partial knowledge and unpredictable accident. It satisfies the condition of an auditor for whom political experience is a succession of disclosures to which an elective attention may be paid. The form comports well with our most literal and analytic conceptions of political activity. That is why, even despite the inaccuracies and partialities of television reportage, it would be a mistake to regard the dramatic shaping of political activity as itself necessarily deceptive or logically improper.

The discipline of logic cannot, after all, deal with controversy except by regulating its content and confirming its points of incompatibility. Logic cannot sustain contradiction. But at the genesis and fountainhead of logic was the prefiguring discipline of dialectic, which was at once an investigatory procedure and a dramatic form in which adversary and incompatible viewpoints were organized and explicated. The issue of dialectic was not always victory for one contention and defeat for another. Sometimes it was reconciliation.

8
The Mutability of Rhetoric

———— People have changed. We can begin with that banality because it is the premise of a view of history. No matter how complex, views of history rest ultimately on truisms, on platitudes whispered to the twilight. Yet, it is hard to imagine a more secure foundation for a speculative effort than a general proposition that seems conspicuously true.

Notoriously truisms wither under rigorous examination because their contraries are equally plausible. "Three's a crowd" and "The more the merrier;" "Slow and steady wins the race" and "He who hesitates is lost." The demonstration has been made ad tedium. Appropriately then, the postulate that people have changed has a contrary that also makes perfectly good sense. In fact, the assumption that people have not changed, that the sources, shapes, and ends of human motivation have remained constant through history, is common in rhetorical theory and criticism.

If we assume that there is a persisting human nature, abiding through the perturbations of time, we will be disposed to assimilate the past to our own experience. In rhetoric we would understand the theoretical treatises of other times as addressing issues that we ourselves engage. And we would understand the rhetorical discourses of other times as, at the least, prospective models that we may now emulate.

The assumption of human constancy is beyond refutation. For every datum of evidence that can be advanced against it, another can be advanced in its favor. True, Socrates was an Athenian who lived two millennia ago, but can we not identify that vivid dissenter who emerges from the Platonic dialogues as a man who could take up in our world the same conversations that he had in his own? True, we cannot surrender ourselves to the religious cosmology of *Oedipus Rex* in the way that Sophocles' contemporaries did, but does the drama not move us to confront a perennial human condition? Freud thought so. This interplay of affirmation and denial could go on forever, for the assumption of an immutable human nature will not finally be confirmed or disconfirmed by mere facts. Neither that assumption nor its contrary is drawn from facts. Rather, each is a perspective that can organize facts, but that must be justified, if at all, on moral or prudential grounds. The issue attending such a perspective is more its efficacy than its accuracy.

If, in contemplating the history of rhetorical activity, we assume that people have changed, that there have been "radical discontinuities in the history of consciousness,"[1] we are brought to the question of whether the functions of rhetoric have altered over time. The question is elusive, and what makes it so is its evidentiary perplexity. We cannot expect that discourses themselves would provide sufficient information for answering the question. If an instrument is put to some secondary use, and that use eventually comes to supersede or perhaps even to replace the primary use, the instrument itself may not change at all. One could look at the history of a technique and find stability in its form when, in fact, the people who used the technique had been much changed by it and in turn had changed their use of it.

The question of whether the functions of rhetoric have undergone historical change has, then, no obvious way of being answered. We have available to us, for investigatory purposes, an uncountable number of discourses from the past, but our question is not about the properties of those discourses. We have, rather, asked a question about their functions. We are not inquiring about the characteristics of communications; we are instead inquiring about the kinds of experience associated with communications.

The functions of rhetoric are not available to us for direct observation. Those functions are in the experiential realm. They are subcutaneous. I know how some rhetorical communications affect me because I experience the effects; but that you too have similar experiences is, for me, no more than a working hypothesis. It is a necessary and sometimes even powerful hypothesis, but I cannot know about your experiences as I know about my own. I can only observe their symptoms. We extend that same indirect observation to all people in all places and ages when we assume that they reacted to persuasion as we react, but we lack definitive confirmation of that assumption. We have in the alluvium of time the relics of men and women now dead, memorials of their consciousness; but no one of us has ever observed the experience of another person in its full sensate measure.

The evidence that is available concerning the functions of rhetoric is reflectional and technically superficial. Because the inaccessibility of others' rhetorical experience limits us to symptoms of a subject that are not quite the subject itself, our inquiry is fated to indirection. It is an essay in what Foucault has termed "the archeology of knowledge" (*l'archéologie du savoir*), to distinguish it from the history of ideas.[2]

Our conventional assumption is that people have always stood in roughly the same relationship to persuasive messages as we; that, mutatis mutandis, people have always been disposed to understand and respond in similar ways. Let us stand the conventional assumption on its head. Let us assume that the ways in which auditors experience rhetorical communication have altered over time, and then let us consider whether evidence supporting such an assumption is capable of forming itself into a coherent account with explanatory power.

As we explore the hypothesis that the functions of rhetoric have changed over time, we should not expect those changes to have been quick. On the contrary, our knowledge of our personal histories suggests that functional change is more likely to be gradual than precipitous, a matter of metamorphosis rather than sudden mutation. The seed of a new response is likely to lie inchoate among the old responses; otherwise, the new would be inexplicable. Therefore our inquiry cannot profit from comparing one moment to the next. The historic change we seek would be too finely graduated for microscopy, ironic as that may seem. The field is not the blade of grass, the face is not the freckle. If we hope to determine whether change has occurred, we have to bring side by side epochs that are remote from one another, and ignore their intervening transitions.

Moreover, we must bear in mind throughout our exploration that we have, in order to inspect them, arrested periods of time that were in fact fluidly transitory. Whether we are looking at the sixth century B.C. or the last century or even the last week, we are treating as fixed and autonomous a flow of time that was continuous with what came before and after it. Any moment in history is a transitional moment: that qualification must be understood as obtaining in anything anyone says about it.

The first phase of the history of rhetoric is, of course, coeval with classical antiquity. There can be no doubt that people engaged in rhetorical transactions before the classical period. They must have sold their goods, praised their monarchs, courted their sweethearts, supplicated their gods. They wheedled, argued, litigated, seduced, slandered, and inspired. What they evidently did not do was to comprehend these diverse activities as particular expressions of a general linguistic method. The first recognition we know of the persuasive uses of language as embodying a special facility and constituting therefore a potential art dates from Greek antiquity, and we are left with an extensive rhetorical literature from that time.

If we had to find a single property of those rhetorics of antiquity—some characteristic other than the sheer genius of some of them—that marked them as distinctive from our own perspective, that quality might well be their relative intimacy. It is true that the Athens of Gorgias or of Demosthenes was worldly, informed, and sophisticated, and that it presented a rich variety of human types and an ample range of fateful choices, especially if we compare Athens to a more insular community—the Menominee Indian tribe, for example. Yet the rhetorics of the time—those compendia of the ways in which people acquired convictions and, implicatively, those inventories of the sorts of convictions available to them—reveal a closer-knit society than our own, and a more attenuated range of relations between that society and each of its members.

The more nearly tribal character of this consciousness is manifest in the most celebrated theoretical treatise from that epoch, Aristotle's *Rhetoric*. Aristotle took extraordinary pains to make his conception of the enthymeme central in accounting for rhetorical influence. The enthymeme was for Aristotle "the very body and substance of persuasion," and this view requires that all members of an audience share with the rhetor who addresses them an inventory of presuppositions on which the rhetor's arguments are predicated.[3] These presuppositions had to be interpreted in similar ways by all of the parties to a rhetorical transaction and held by them with roughly equal degrees of commitment; otherwise enthymemes could not have the force we must associate with "the very body and substance of persuasion." We do not find in Aristotle, or in other writers of his time, the notion that enthymematic major premises would vary from audience to audience in Athens. Groups of people were acknowledged to be different from one another, of course, but their diversity was a matter of circumstance or of age.[4] There is nowhere in ancient rhetoric the claim that audiences could vary in the fundamental values with which they apprehended rhetorical proofs. The ancients speculated on the origins of language, but they were not concerned with the "problem of communication." The ancients experienced and understood factionalism, but they nowhere hint at ideological conflict.[5] All of these data point to the more socially cohesive character of their consciousness: to their implicit constrictions on individual or subcultural variety, and to the silent reservoir of consensus that their rhetorical transactions assumed.

Viewing the ancients now from our long-removed perspective, we know that their tribal heritage—celebrated by them in their festivals and games—was already eroding even during the first emergence of rhetoric as an art. This erosion was glacially slow, and even the most acute of contemporary observers were scarcely aware of it, but in retrospect it seems inexorable. Finally, centuries later, after the Christianization of the West, it was no longer possible to think of the European consciousness as communal. The substructure of rhetorical activity had changed.

Three aspects of that change especially solicit our attention. First, the rise of Christianity—its nearly universal triumph in Europe—altered by intensification the importance of believing itself, and thereby raised the importance to people of rhetorical transactions. Second, Christianity altered by extension the degree to which people experienced themselves as individuals, and thereby changed the tone and techniques of rhetorical transactions. And third, Christianity altered by displacement the inventory of presuppositions that people unquestioningly accepted, and thereby became, for the period of its hegemony, the substantive foundation of rhetorical transactions.

The first of those three aspects of change—the intensification of the importance of believing—is fundamental to the way in which Christianity took hold of the Western mind. Erich Kahler, writing of the Pauline influence, described the contrast between pre-Christian communal consciousness and the post-Christian orientation:

> The new covenant between man and God was founded, as far as man was concerned, not on good works but on faith, as far as God was concerned, not on an impersonal law but on personal grace. This was the necessary prerequisite for unifying the people of all the different tribes in one creed that was not their own hereditary, innate religion. It meant a revolution in religion itself and the foundation of a world religion. It meant the abolishment of religion in its essential character, the transformation of religion into creed, into profession of belief. True religion was not founded on mere belief. It was not something one could accept and profess voluntarily and abandon voluntarily. It was a vital, biological bond, rooted in the very ex-

istence of man. It was identical with the ancestral, the tribal bond, it connected the human being with the essence of the tribe and he could free himself of it no more than of his ancestral generations, of his ethnic character. The new, Christian God was an outward God, one who came to men, appealed to them in their quality of human beings only, and with whom men were connected by a bond of confidence, of belief only.[6]

Pauline Christianity fully realized a conception that before had been alien to the Greco-Roman tradition and that had appeared only sporadically and controversially in the Hebraic tradition. It was a conception that emerged in the confluence of those two traditions in the form of evangelical Christianity. The conception was that the individual's belief determined the individual's destiny.

Christianity confirmed the primacy of belief. It promised eternal bliss as the reward for believing—truly believing—its own proffered truths, and it guaranteed eternal torment for disbelieving them. For the first time in Western history, one's cosmic fate became the product of one's convictions. This radical alteration of consciousness, once fixed, came in time to function archetypally: capable of detachment not only from sectarian tenets but even from religion itself, imposing its form even on the most secular of ideologies. Such intensification in the importance of believing is a pervasive residue of Christianity.

Of the uncountable consequences to rhetorical activity of this historic change, one was illumined by Robert King Merton's old and classic study of the Kate Smith war bond campaign.[7] Merton and his associates interviewed some of the people who had been influenced by Kate Smith, a radio celebrity of the 1940s, to purchase bonds during the Second World War. The subjects, asked to account for their having been persuaded by Kate Smith, remarked on her sincerity as the most influential characteristic of her campaign.

Among the moral achievements of which humankind is capable, surely sincerity would have to be regarded as, at best, among the most modest. As a subordinate form of truthfulness, sincerity seems rather an obligation than a positive good, rather a requirement than a virtue. Yet Kate Smith appeared to be sincere to people, and so she was able to sell vast amounts of war bonds. Whence sincerity? How has it come to be regarded as a positive merit? And why is its opposite—hypocrisy—so heinous a vice? The answers to those questions give us some measure of the ramifications of the Christian emphasis on believing.

Hypocrisy does not appear in literature as an object of serious opprobrium until the medieval period. We have in the extant literature of classical antiquity no character like Tartuffe. Certainly there are personae in ancient literature whose behavior is at variance from their professions. The Socrates character in *Clouds* is a pretentious windbag, and the "parasite" character in Plautus is a wily rogue, but there is nothing sinister about these characters. They are too ridiculous to be apprehended as wicked. Hypocrisy was not a major vice to the ancients. They seemed rather to regard it as a violation of simple propriety—almost an aesthetic offence, like dressing eccentrically or eating sloppily. It was a laughable affront rather than a breach of morality, more a frailty than a transgression. Later, after the triumph of Christianity, hypocrisy became an iniquity, a particularly repugnant corruption, and, naturally enough, sincerity came to be a major virtue.

Such changes in moral perspective do not occur casually. When a pair of contrasting behaviors evolves from the bland economy of decorum to become important pivots of moral judgment, we may legitimately suspect that something important has happened to the culture in which this moral change has occurred, something behind the change, propelling it and giving it psychological sanction. Christianity's influence on the form and centrality of belief would account for that change.

Only when belief is detached from behavior, when the seam binding the two has come unraveled, can issues of sincerity and hypocrisy arise.[8] One of the conditions of tribal existence is that belief and behavior are more nearly unitary. The very distinction between an inner life that can be associated with belief and a social life of overt behavior is, in the tribal ambience, preempted by a received consensual tradition. The choices to be made within a tribe and, hence, the professions that can be betrayed present themselves to us as few and superficial, and even they rest on the secure foundation of a communal faith. To bring into question a tenet of that faith could only be the work of some feral deviant: a genius or a lunatic. For virtually anyone else, questioning the tribal heritage would be impossible because it would involve a psychological independence and social detachment for which tribal experience simply does not provide the resources.[9]

The reflexive analysis that we associate with Cartesian doubt—the extension of skepticism to the point that it must finally acknowledge itself as a certitude or else cancel thought entirely—appears to be the ultimate principled development of individuality. And the varieties of malaise that accompany that corrosive self-consciousness do not afflict one who is absorbed within the communal matrix.

With the rise of Christianity, belief and behavior, in the forms respectively of faith and works, were cleanly separated. A god was enthroned who could look into the soul and see his commandments violated in that secret place, and who could therefore enforce distinctively his ordinances on each moiety of the bifurcation. At last there had to be a moral adjustment to this new fissure in the human personality, and in the course of it, sincerity and hypocrisy assumed their modern status.

The disparity between belief and behavior accompanying and accelerated by the rise of Christianity seems to have reached a crisis in the nineteenth century, when virtually every aspect of moral life was apprehended in the dichotomous terms of appearance and reality. Some of the great speculative minds of the period—notably Marx and Freud—devoted themselves to stripping away veils of gentility for access to a reality that was disguised, concealed, suppressed. This lust for disclosure, together with its subtle but constant solicitation to paranoia, has abided with undiminished power for over a hundred years now. It has acquired the expressive autonomy and recurring significance of a rhetorical form.

Another literary possibility created by the disparity between belief and behavior is the audacious defiance of orthodoxies, supremely illustrated by the works of the Marquis de Sade. Both *Justine* and *La Philosophie dans le boudoir* are structured into oscillating episodes of salacity and iconoclastic preachments, so that the reader is confronted with scenes that defy behavioral proprieties alternating with scenes that defy convictional proprieties. The repudiation of orthodoxy is complete, but the author is careful to maintain in the structure of his work the distinction between behavior and belief, together with the implication that the two domains are subject to different moral regulations. Thus the character Justine sustains her subjective purity and her allegiance to conventional pieties while, behaviorally, she leaves hardly a single sexual taboo unviolated.

Of course no consideration of the schism's influence can omit the great, introspective, conscience-ridden heroes of post-Renaissance literature from Hamlet to Raskolnikov. Each is afflicted by a malign discrepancy between belief and behavior, and each is in quest of a healing reconciliation. In *Hamlet* the consummation is a deed; in *Crime and Punishment* it is a conviction. But it is precisely the need to integrate deed with conviction that propels dramatic movement in both works.

The emergence of fanaticism was another symptom of the intensification of concern with believing that accompanied the rise of Christianity. Fanaticism designates a psychological condition: a way of believing, but not a belief. To call a person a fanatic is to suggest nothing about the subjects that are fanatically believed, either personal, religious, or political. A fanatic may be of the Right or the Left, may be Hindu or Muslim, Christian or Jewish, atheistic or deistic. To know only that a person is fanatical is to know nothing of what that person believes. It is, however, to know *how* that person believes: it is to know that, irrespective of what the convictions are, they are held stubbornly, ardently, and undoubtingly. Most menacing of all, we expect from the fanatic a certain perverse probity. One who pursues interest can be swayed. Venality may be bribed, ambition flattered, passion seduced; but there is a tenaciously selfless dedication in the fanatic. The idée fixe is the consuming motive. The fanatic casts on all blandishments a cold, reptilian eye.

The possibility of fanaticism does not appear in any of the rhetorical theories of the ancients. However Dionysian some of their art and ritual, their rhetorical transactions seemed thoroughly Apollonian. Very much to this point is the endearing legend of Aristides the Just who so wearied his compatriots with the obstinacy of his rectitude that they drove him into exile. His virtue was fanatical, hence unbearable.

Not even the martyrdom of Socrates provides evidence of fanaticism in antiquity. His persecutors seem to have been men of inflexible conventionality: narrow, unimaginative, perhaps indifferent to ideas: early patriots defending the status quo. And certainly Socrates himself was no fanatic. Ironists never are.[10]

Fanaticism is a form of believing that is related to certain forms of persuasion. Fanaticism is the inward and psychological state associated with an outward and verbal incitement. To say, therefore, that fanaticism became more common in the West during the Christian era is to say that a certain attitude toward belief emerged then, and with it a certain attitude toward the acquisition of belief. Those are the sorts of attitudes that are central to the discipline of rhetoric.

There was another historical change complicatedly connected to the shifts in the importance of belief and believing. It too was a change in emphasis, and it concerned the degree to which people experienced themselves as individuals. Erich Kahler, referring to the later Roman Empire, noted it: "The fundamental innovation of this whole epoch is that the individual stands forth, the lonely private individual with all his ancestral, tribal bonds broken off, the earthly individual standing on his own feet, under the vast sky of universality. And this is the turning point of human history."[11]

The further back before the Christian era we project our vision, the more attenuated we see the scope afforded to individual experience and action. Religious convictions, which were pervasive, were not a subject of individual choice. They were, as Kahler suggested, a communal heritage. They were unchallengeable because a tribal condition does not supply the psychological resources for iconoclasm. One can discern the shadow of this unity even in so late and unlikely a source as Aristotle's *Poetics*, where *hamartia*—the tragic flaw—is hubris: willful self-assertiveness, a crude excess of ego.

The presuppositions of the tribe could not be questioned or challenged less because of arbitrary prohibitions than because such defiance requires an identity, an ego, an individual who is sufficiently divorced from those presuppositions to be critical of them, and such autonomous identities were only just beginning to emerge when the first rhetorics were being composed. Christianity, however, forced unprecedented choices. One could no longer be at peace with the cosmic order simply by belonging to a community with its own gods. The choice was now with the individual. He had to confront his god alone and be judged by his god alone. The ego was born, and with it a terrible solitude.

Friedrich Solmsen, commenting especially on the *Nicomachean Ethics* and the *Politics*, noted the incipient presence of individuality in Aristotle:

> With all his intense concern about the efficient operation of the political machinery, with all his strong and very Hellenic feeling about a man's duty to his community, Aristotle yet has no doubt that a person's happiness and the true values of his life lie outside the realm of public activity. We have seen how much this view corresponds to tendencies that had been there, had been strong, had increased in strength during several generations. But we may with equal right look at these Aristotelian doctrines as a vision anticipating developments of the future.[12]

Bruno Snell, who argued that the "cognizance of individuality and the establishment of the polis are contemporary events," located the first historic evidence of individuality in the poet Archilochus, the putative inventor of the monodic lyric, who lived in the first half of the seventh century, B.C. Snell observed of Archilochus and of the later lyrists Sappho and Anacreon:

> In the expression of their private sentiments and demands the early lyrists try to reproduce those moments in which the individual is all of a sudden snatched out of the broad stream of life, when he senses that he is cut off from the ever-green tree of universal growth. Such are the moments which furnish man with his first glimpse of the soul. This new personal soul is not yet by any means the foundation for all feelings and emotions; it is merely the source of the reactions which set in when the feelings are blocked.[13]

Each generation of us must now perform for itself an act of reconstruction to understand why and how ethics and politics were conjoined in the ancient philosophers. Their vision does not come easily to us. We do not live in a world in which the mandates governing individual behavior dissolve into a communal network. Each of us is conscious of the self and posits society as a necessary abstraction. But to the ancients, the community had a more vivid reality, and the individual was more nearly an abstraction.

These changes in Western consciousness crystallized in religious form, but they became archetypal patterns of perception and cognition. As such, they extended into nonreligious areas, most notably into politics. As a result of the evangelical emphasis on faith over works, the operation of rhetorical discourse in people's lives became immeasurably more influential than it had been in classical antiquity. The question of what to believe became more prominent, more pressing, and in a sense more oppressive than it had ever been.

Christianity altered the intensity and scope of believing, but it did perpetrate for a long time an inventory of shared presuppositions, and thereby served as a psychological substitute for tribal mythopoesis. The rise of Christianity represented the triumph of a single myth—the most successful ideological hegemony the world has yet known. For a variety of reasons, however, Christianity seemed to have reached an apogee of strength at some point prior to the Renaissance, and since then its rivals have proliferated as its rhetorical monopoly has disintegrated. Other loyalties came to centrality in people's lives; other idioms of collective identity formed their language. As Ian Watt observed, "In the sixteenth century the Reformation and the rise of national states decisively challenged the substantial social homogeneity of medieval Christendom, and in the famous words of Maitland, 'for the first time, the Absolute State faced the Absolute Individual.'"[14]

We are left, then, with two major increments that bear noting: one is the enhancement of individual commitment since the great rhetorical treatises of antiquity were composed—the intensification of the importance of making up one's mind. The second increment is the condition of competing ideologies vying for our allegiance—a result of the decline of Christianity's hegemony. Like Christianity, these ideologies often make claims of universality and exclusivity, so that they represent themselves as imperative and mutually exclusive choices.[15]

Those two increments may have a more direct relationship with one another than their common origin in a single historical movement. If, as a result of Pauline Christianity, the acceptance of a belief became more crucial in human experience and made claims on a higher proportion of energy, attention, and concern than it had in the pre-Christian era, there might well arise from that condition a strong desire for sufficiently diverse and compelling subjects of belief to correspond to and warrant the centrality of commitment itself. In sum, one should expect, in response to the enhanced importance of believing, a correlative enhancement in the sphere of ideology. Just as the development of a special taste seems to encourage a proliferation of refinements satisfying that taste, so the acquisition of an appetite for believing could have encouraged a multiplication of beliefs, perhaps initially confined to theological matters, but increasingly encompassing with the passage of time until, as now, the realm of the contingent becomes virtually coterminous with the life of the mind.

This relationship between the exaltation of commitment and the variegation of beliefs must have become reciprocal, for the very availability of competing sects and ideologies, each urging its imperative claims, would induce individuals to become more acutely conscious of their ability to make commitments and encourage them to exercise it more. Behind this account is the premise that the capacity for embracing convictions is innately dormant and that it will be activated only by a stimulus—typically a claim made on the individual's credulity. A proposition central to this essay is that rhetorical propensities are neither spontaneous nor enduring. They are the products of cultural conditions: social epiphenomena that will be historically fluctuant with the society itself.

For the very reason that rhetorical propensities are culturally dependent, the present diagnosis of some effects of Christianity on rhetorical practice can itself be credited with only, at best, a transient validity. The ideologies that compete for our allegiance have differing estimates of the importance of believing, differing commitments to commitment itself. We cannot assume that the possibilities of rhetorical activity have all been realized, much less exhausted. History does not end with us. History has a future.

Patently, these pages have scarcely made a beginning of exploring the hypothesis that people have changed in ways that affect rhetoric. The subject merits a systematic investigation of much greater magnitude. Such a project would confront the evidentiary problems attendant on any investigation of the experiential realm, and it would be inhibited, just as the present effort is, by the remarkable poverty of our vocabulary about rhetorical experience. If, undefeated by those difficulties, an inquiry could proceed, its issue would be to subordinate the study of rhetoric to the history of consciousness.

At least two consequences may be anticipated from that subordination. One, already familiar, would be to promote a rigorously contextual view of rhetorical theories of the past—to understand them as time-bound. That perspective would allow us neither to presume the current accuracy of a past rhetorical theory nor to discredit it for its current inaccuracy. It would oblige us instead to reserve the possibility that a theory of rhetoric may speak for its time, that it may retrieve for us a *mentalité*, long vanished, that it faithfully reflects.

A second consequence of subordinating the study of rhetoric to the history of consciousness would be to render rhetorical theory a product of rhetorical criticism. The referent of theory would shift from the processes by which people and ideas are mutually adjusted[16] to the characteristics and functions of discourses that survive from the past. So conceived, a rhetorical theory would not then be an abstract or ideal model of a rhetorical transaction. Rather, it would be a general interpretation of a body of rhetorical transactions that had actually occurred. Rhetorical theory would be occupied with disclosing relationships among discourses and between discourses and their historical circumstances. Its probable form would be a system of rhetorical genres, contextually and developmentally comprehended.

This consideration of the mutability of rhetoric has been predicated, necessarily, on the mutability of consciousness itself. It seems unavoidable that such an effort at synopsis would be, as this one has been, abstract. The character of rhetoric is better sought in specific transactions: in a discourse or a set of discourses, in a campaign or a persuasive movement, in an event with a beginning and an end. But those discrete transactions, taken together, may themselves have an aggregated shape, an intricate and elusive collective design that can be revelatory of human experience. That enigmatic pattern will be elicited—if it can be elicited at all—only by the most penetrating critical examination of specific rhetorical artifacts. Thus this essay, which began with one banality, can end with another—with, indeed, the most bromidic peroration available to scholarly publication: Further research is needed.

We always need further research. In that at least, people have not changed.

Notes

Introduction: Rhetoric as Critique

1. Lionel Trilling, *The Liberal Imagination: Essays on Literature and Society* (Garden City, NY: Doubleday & Co., 1953), p. 26

2. Walter Jackson Bate, *Criticism: The Major Texts* (New York: Harcourt, Brace & World, 1952), p. 277.

3. Illuminating rhetorical critiques have been written about works of scientific theory and about popularizations of science. But the experimental report appearing, for example, in *Physical Review* is impervious to rhetorical criticism. A critic confronting such a document could do no more than report the obvious: that it is organized according to a certain formula, or that it extensively employs a specialized vocabulary, or that it comports with certain conventions of the discipline. These are observations known to every first-year graduate student in physics. If such banalities qualify as rhetorical criticism, then Monsieur Jourdain's discovery that he spoke in prose constitutes stylistic analysis.

4. Aristotle, *Nicomachean Ethics* 6.1140a20.

5. Richard Hofstadter, *The Paranoid Style in American Politics* (New York: Alfred A. Knopf, 1967), esp. pp. 35–38.

Chapter 1. Idioms of Social Identity

1. E. David Cronon, *Black Moses: The Story of Marcus Garvey and the Universal Negro Improvement Association* (1955; reprint, Madison: University of Wisconsin Press, 1969), pp. 186–87.

2. Ibid., pp. 188–95.

3. See: Malcolm X's 3 April 1964 version of "The Ballot or the Bullet" in *Malcolm X Speaks*, ed. George Breitman (New York: Grove, 1965), pp. 23–44, or, in the same source, his "Letter" from Accra, Ghana, pp. 62–63; also, Stokely Carmichael's Detroit speech of 30 July 1966, an edited transcription of which appears in Robert L. Scott and Wayne Brockriede, *The Rhetoric of Black Power* (New York: Harper & Row, 1969), pp. 85–95.

"I have a Dream" is, of course, an appeal for national reconciliation. The anthem of King's movement, "We Shall Overcome," was echoed twice in Johnson's speech.

4. There have been proposals that some section of the United States be reserved for exclusively black settlement. For example, the African Blood Brotherhood contemplated the establishment of a black republic somewhere in the South. (See Theodore G. Vincent, *Black Power and the Garvey Movement* [San Francisco: Ramparts Press, 1972], pp. 18, 74–85.) The more popular, recurrent, and influential proposal, however, has been the separate development of black economic enterprises, encouraged by figures as diverse as Booker T. Washington, Marcus Garvey, Malcolm X, and Richard Nixon. Garvey especially emphasized the distinctive cultural identity that such economic independence would support, a theme that was also important to Malcolm X.

5. Quoted in Irwin Ross, *The Loneliest Campaign* (New York: New American Library, 1968), pp. 231–32. The compatibility between Southern sectionalism and racism was well illustrated in the keynote address to the States Rights party's 1948 convention given by former Governor Frank M. Dixon of Alabama. Dixon characterized Truman's civil rights proposals as an attempt "to reduce us to the status of a mongrel, inferior race, mixed in blood, our Anglo-Saxon heritage a mockery." Ross, p. 131.

6. Jody Carlson, *George C. Wallace and the Politics of Powerlessness: The Wallace Campaigns for the Presidency, 1964–1976* (New Brunswick: Transaction Books, 1981), pp. 5, 85.

Although Wallace's electoral base was in the south, his 1964 and 1968 presidential candidacies drew substantial support in northern industrial areas. Herbert S. Parmet has noted, "As the racial conflicts of the mid-sixties spread to the North, so did Wallace's message, touching a nerve that resonated with nonsouthern, working-class whites." *Richard Nixon and His America* (Boston: Little, Brown & Co., 1990), p. 497.

In the 1972 primary campaign when Wallace ran for the Democratic nomination, he entered fourteen primaries before he was shot, and got a million and a half more votes than any of his rivals.

7. The account below of "kind" and "kindness" provides further material for the explication of Tennessee Williams's brilliantly multivalent line.

8. "Gorbachev and his colleagues [in the Politburo] think of themselves as Soviet men for whom ethnicity remains a kind of 'survival of the past,' doomed according to their ideology to wither away. Moreover, they tend to approach politics with the assumption that all other Soviet citizens should recognize that the reforms that will undoubtedly benefit all should not be limited by ethnic demands benefiting a relative few." Paul A. Goble, "Mikhail Gorbachev's Myopic Vision of His Country," *Washington Post National Weekly Edition,* 2–8 April 1990, p. 23.

9. Adolf Hitler, Speech in Berlin, 30 January 1937, published in *Voelkischer Beobachter,* 31 January 1937. Reprinted in *Hitler's Words,* ed. Gordon W. Prange (Washington, DC: American Council on Public Affairs, 1944).

10. As early as 1923, and repeatedly during the subsequent decade, Hitler was advocating a consolidated Germany and accusing a hostile France of cultivating sectionalism within Germany. See, for example, his speech in Munich of 4 May 1923, published in *Voelkischer Beobachter,* 6–7 May 1923, or the Munich speech of 27 March 1924, published in the same source on 28 March 1924.

In an important address to the Reichstag early in his chancellorship, Hitler said: "The strength of the national-socialist party lies in the fact that, even during its inner construction, it never forgot the roots of its existence. It was not founded for individual states with their individual populations, but for the German nation and the German people." He went on to say of the German states and their princely dynasties, "Even if this family power policy made use of slumbering racial characteristics, it did not enhance the importance of those races in the eyes of the world or enrich their capacities to live, but rather condemned them in general to an undignified insignificance." *Address of January 30, 1934* (Berlin: Reichsdruckerei, 1934), p. 20.

11. See Teun A. van Dijk, *Communicating Racism: Ethnic Prejudice in Thought and Talk* (Newbury Park: Sage, 1987), pp. 180–249; and Vincent, *Black Power,* esp. pp. 117–19.

12. C. T. Onions, ed., *The Oxford Dictionary of English Etymology* (Oxford: Oxford University Press, 1966), p. v.

13. David Remnick reported from Vilnius: "Lithuanian is the language of the day, and residents speak Russian reluctantly and, very often, badly. On Sunday mornings, Lithuanian television has begun broadcasting Catholic mass on a new program, 'Glory to Christ.' Young people have quit the Communist youth groups, Young Pio-

neers and Young Communist League in droves and are joining the Scouts—a kind of junior Sajudis [the name of the Lithuanian independence movement]. Dozens of streets have been changed back to their old Lithuanian names. Just recently, Lenin Street, where Sajudis has its headquarters, became Gedimanis Street, named for an ancient Lithuanian patriarch." *Washington Post National Weekly Edition*, 21–27 August 1989, p. 16.

14. "Rarely are we met with a challenge, not to our growth or abundance, our welfare or our security, but rather to the values and the purposes and the meaning of our beloved Nation.

"The issue of equal rights for American Negroes is such an issue. And should we defeat every enemy, should we double our wealth and conquer the stars, and still be unequal to this issue, then we will have failed as a people and as a nation."

15. Repeatedly throughout his political career, Hitler associated his vision of Germany with the divine will. A typical passage occurred in a speech given in Berlin on 1 May 1935: "You are members of one people and . . . you are so not by human will but by God's will. It was He who made us members of this nation, He who gave us our mother tongue." *Völkischer Beobachter*, 2 May 1935.

16. Without meaning to be defiant, I have to remind the reader who would dissent from this argument that such a dissent, in effect, absolves me of responsibility for being wrong. If people are not responsible for their convictions, then how can I be responsible for mine? And if I am responsible for mine, then there must be other people who are responsible for theirs. If no one is responsible for his or her belief, then why should any belief (including the present one) ever be objected to? Do people object to other "natural" phenomena? Has the reader objected to a storm or an earthquake? If so, to whom?

17. Clifford Geertz, "The Integrative Revolution," *The Interpretation of Cultures* (New York: Basic Books, 1973), p. 259. See also Edward Shils, "Primordial, Personal, Sacred and Civil Ties," *British Journal of Sociology* 8 (1957): 130–45.

18. See, for example, the report of David Remnick in the *Washington Post National Weekly Edition*, 7–13 August 1989, pp. 17–18.

19. Ibid., p. 18; and 21–27 August 1989, p. 17. See also reports by Celestine Bohlen in the *New York Times*, 15 May 1990, pp. 1 and 8; and 16 May 1990, pp. 1 and 15.

Chapter 2. Secrecy and Disclosure as Rhetorical Forms

1. Quintilian, *Institutio Oratoria* 2.20.7. An ancient passion for irony was fulfilled in the conception of the two great disciplines con-

cerned with oppositions, rhetoric and dialectic, as themselves opposed.

2. The method pursued here—if "method" is not too pretentious a term for this effort—may remind some readers of the analyses of "categorical opposites drawn from everyday experience" conducted by Claude Levi-Strauss in, for example, his investigations of the raw and the cooked, the fresh and the rotten, the moist and the parched. See Claude Lévi-Strauss, *Le Cru et le Cuit* (Paris: Plon, 1964); translated by John and Doreen Weightman as *The Raw and the Cooked* (New York: Harper & Row, 1969; paperback edition published by the University of Chicago Press). The present inquiry is unrelated to those in structuralist anthropology except for the most superficial similarities. This investigation is not concerned with cultural differences or with cross-cultural forms. Rhetorical in its orientation, it is solely occupied with Western culture, focused on the forms of belief as they are expressed in discourse, and predicated on the suspicion that stark contrasts in the language are symptomatic of more elaborate but equally antipodal bifurcations in beliefs. The inquiry may be interpreted as an amplification of the author's comments on rhetorical compatibility in *Rhetorical Criticism: A Study in Method* (Madison: University of Wisconsin Press, 1978), pp. 165–76.

3. This mode of discussion, based on Aristotelian rhetoric, appears to be a sustained spatial metaphor. It represents verbal activity as occupying a certain space and as impinging on adjoining spaces where other abstract activities are represented as occurring. But simply because, at least casually considered, the discussion seems to be metaphorical, one should not be too confident that the discussion is therefore inferior to some other, hypothetically literal account that may, in principle, be possible. Such modesty is required by the Kantian dispensation that makes space a category of thought and therefore essential to reason. Spatiality would thus be not really figurative, but rather an indispensable component of one's very mind and thereby as literal as it is possible to be. Wittgenstein's advice is the famous concluding sentence of *Tractatus Logico-Philosophicus:* "Whereof one cannot speak, thereof one must be silent."

4. "Rhetorical form" here refers to a pattern by which commitments are solicited. Such a form would be significant in the sense examined by Suzanne Langer in *Philosophy in a New Key* (New York: New American Library, 1948), esp. pp. 75–94.

5. Tzvetan Todorov, *The Poetics of Prose*, trans. Richard Howard (Ithaca: Cornell University Press, 1977), p. 129.

6. David Grossvogel, *Mystery and Its Fictions: From Oedipus to Agatha Christie* (Baltimore: Johns Hopkins University Press, 1979), p. 4.

7. Hannah Arendt, *The Origins of Totalitarianism* (New York: Harcourt Brace & World, 1951), esp. pp. 341–51.

8. Vincent Bugliosi with Curt Gentry, *Helter Skelter* (New York: W. W. Norton, 1974), pp. 324–31.

9. Frank Kermode, *The Genesis of Secrecy* (Cambridge: Harvard University Press, 1979), p. 144.

10. See J. Hillis Miller, "Stevens' Rock and Criticism as Cure, II," *Georgia Review* 30 (Summer 1976): 333; Vincent B. Leitch, "The Lateral Dance: The Deconstructive Criticism of J. Hillis Miller," *Critical Inquiry* 6 (Summer 1980): 605; Geoffrey Hartman, *The Fate of Reading* (Chicago: University of Chicago Press, 1975), p. 271.

11. *Robert Oppenheimer: Letters and Recollections,* ed. Alice Kimball Smith and Charles Weiner (Cambridge: Harvard University Press, 1980), pp. 317–18. The speech was given on 2 November 1945.

12. Herbert Butterfield, *The Origins of Modern Science, 1300–1800* (London: G. Bell & Sons, 1962), p. 112.

13. "We do not regard an analysis as at an end until all the obscurities of the case are cleared up, the gaps in the patient's memory filled in, the precipitating causes of the repression discovered." Sigmund Freud, *Introductory Lectures on Psychoanalysis,* trans. and ed. James Strachey (New York: W. W. Norton, 1977), pp. 452–53. See also pp. 454–55.

14. In "The Defence Neuro-Psychoses," *Collected Papers of Sigmund Freud,* 5 vols. (London: Hogarth Press, 1949), 1:165. Freud is explicit in finding the origins of social emotions in private affects. And his choice of imagery is significant in basing the difference between "nervous health and neurosis" on "the relative sizes of the quota of energy that remains free and of that which is bound by repression." Freud, *Introductory Lectures,* p. 457. See also Philip Rieff, *Freud: The Mind of the Moralist* (New York: Doubleday, 1961), p. 278.

15. Rieff puts the matter well: "However much Freudianism may itself function as an ideology, it inculcates . . . skepticism about all ideologies except those of the private life. Psychoanalysis is the doctrine of the private man defending himself against public encroachment." Rieff, *Freud,* p. 278.

16. Richard Hofstadter, *The Paranoid Style in American Politics* (New York: Alfred A. Knopf, 1967), esp. pp. 3–40.

17. Perry Miller counts in the hundreds the number of nineteenth-century sermons in America that "called the roll . . . of the great kingdoms which had perished—Chaldea, Egypt, Greece, Rome—" because they had not relied on the "conservative qualities" of the Christian religion. Miller, *The Life of the Mind in America* (New York: Harcourt Brace & World, 1965, pp. 70–71.

Such monitory calling of the roll is still with us, as is the converse allusion to the historical record: history as a source of precedent and inspiration. Thucydides' reconstruction of Pericles' Funeral Oration and its descendent, Lincoln's Gettysburg Address, are two masterpieces in that latter tradition, which is renewed during every patriotic holiday.

18. Witold Rybczynski, *Home: A Short History* (New York: Viking Penguin, 1986), p. 35.

19. Ibid., p. 39.

20. The relationship between secrecy and property has etymological roots: "'Proper,' 'propriety,' and 'property' relate to *pro privo* in Latin and thus to 'privacy.'" Sissela Bok, *Secrets: On the Ethics of Concealment and Revelation* (New York: Random House, 1984), p. 290.

21. S. I. Iutkevich, et al., eds., *Kinoslovar' v dvukh tomakh* (Moscow: Sovetskaia entsiklopediia, 1966), 1:448.

22. *Craig v. Harney,* 331 U.S. 367, 374 (1947).

23. Patricia Fumerton, "'Secret' Arts: Elizabethan Miniatures and Sonnets," *Representations* 15 (Summer 1986): 57–97.

24. Karl Marx and Friedrich Engles, *The German Ideology, Parts I and III* (New York: International Publishers, 1939), pp. 22–43.

25. Vincent Canby, *New York Times,* 21 March 1982, p. 17.

26. Siegfried Kracauer, *From Caligari to Hitler: A Psychological Study of the German Film* (Princeton: Princeton University Press, 1947), pp. 19–20.

27. David Stewart Hull, *Film in the Third Reich: A Study of the German Cinema 1933–1945* (Berkeley and Los Angeles: University of California Press, 1969), p. 39.

28. Ibid., p. 194.

29. The condition of being closed is associated also with the circle. Thus it is pertinent to note that a circle motif pervades that great meditation on political mystery, Conrad's *Secret Agent.* The novel's circularities include the circles that Stevie draws, the pun implicit in Stevie's compass, the circle of conspirators, the family circle, the circularity of the Professor's "moral attitude," the reciprocity between thieves and police, the rotundity of Verloc and of Michealis, the different clocks that run in the novel's disruption of sequence, the topic of eternal recurrence, and the theme of revolution itself. The motif is important to the novel's figural cohesion.

30. Testifying on 21 July 1987 before the Joint Committee of the U.S. Congress investigating the Iran-Contra affair, Admiral John Poindexter defended his concealments by saying, "I firmly believe in very tight compartmentation." The term "compartmentation" was borrowed from naval architecture. It is used there to refer to the di-

vision of a submarine or a surface vessel into separate watertight sections or units. The purpose of compartmentation, of course, is to minimize the damage caused by leaks.

31. Lee Strasberg, "The Actor and Himself," *Actors on Acting*, ed. Toby Cole and Helen Krich Chinoy (New York: Crown, 1970), pp. 626–27.

32. Chancellor Bob Jones, Jr., of Bob Jones University told an audience in Norfolk, Nebraska, that he opposed the exploration of space: "God has separated the light and the dark and I believe there may be things in the heavens God doesn't want us to see." Reported in the *Wisconsin State Journal*, 9 July 1984, p. 3.

Chapter 3. Rhetorical Secrets: Rhetorical Mysteries

1. Roger Morris, *Richard Milhous Nixon: The Rise of an American Politician* (New York: Henry Holt & Co., 1990), pp. 806–7.

2. *Thirty Years of Treason: Excerpts from Hearings before the House Committee on Un-American Activities, 1938–1968*, ed. Eric Bentley (New York: Viking, 1971), p. 941.

3. Ibid., p. 270.

4. Among them were James Burnham, who became a theoretician of conservatism; Edward Dmytryk, one of the Hollywood Ten who recanted his earlier defiance of the committee; Elia Kazan, the celebrated theater and film director; and Clifford Odets, the playwright. All, in their testimony before the House Committee on Un-American Activities, expressed repugnance at the secrecy that American adherents to the Communist party were enjoined to observe.

5. Bentley, Afterword to *Thirty Years of Treason*, pp. 944–45.

6. Richard Nixon, *RN: The Memoirs of Richard Nixon* (New York: Grosset & Dunlap, 1978), p. 783.

7. Thomas Babington Macaulay, *Critical and Historical Essays* (Boston: Houghton Mifflin, 1900), 2:334–35.

8. For an insightful view of Reagan's self-disclosure, but one that does not quite coincide with mine, see: Kathleen Hall Jamieson, "Reagan's use of self-disclosure," in *Eloquence in an Electronic Age: The Transformation of Political Speechmaking* (New York: Oxford University Press, 1988), pp. 182–200.

Chapter 4. The Sentimental Style as Escapism

1. Kenneth Burke, *A Grammar of Motives* (New York: Prentice-Hall, 1952), pp. 430–40.

2. Plato, *Phaedrus* 265, 266, 270D; *Philebus* 16–18; *Cratylus* 424C; *Sophist* 226C, 235C, 253ff.; *Politicus* 285Aff.; *Laws* 894A, 936D, 965C.

3. John Humphrey Noyes, *Male Continence* (Oneida, NY: Oneida Community, 1872; reprinted in *Sexual Indulgence and Denial*, New York: Arno Press, 1974).

4. Daniel Webster, "The Bunker Hill Monument," in *American Speeches*, ed. Wayland Maxfield Parish and Marie Hochmuth (New York: Longmans, Green & Co., 1954), pp. 106–7.

Two notable critics of Webster, while alluding to this passage as a "purple patch," defend it as "justified in such a presence and on such a theme." Wilbur Samuel Howell and Hoyt Hopewell Hudson, "Daniel Webster," *A History and Criticism of American Public Address*, ed. William Norwood Brigance, 3 vols. (New York: Russell & Russell, 1960), 2:681. Later in their essay, Howell and Hudson quote a similarly functioning passage from another speech of Webster's and describe it as "typically Websterian as anything he ever said" (pp. 688–89).

Howell and Hudson argue at length and with considerable cogency (pp. 717–33) that Webster was a popular but not really an effective speaker, that especially his deliberative addresses left his audiences unmoved. The disengagement of Webster's audiences can be explained by the unattractiveness of the condition to which his oratory summoned them, by the plasticity that it demanded of them.

5. Collections of nineteenth-century orations abound in examples of the sentimental style. One such collection is Alexander K. McClure's *Famous American Statesmen and Orators* (New York: F. F. Lovell Publishing Co., 1902) in six volumes. Among its specimens which exhibit, in whole or in part, the sentimental style are: Eliphant Nott, "How Are the Mighty Fallen," 2:308–35; Henry Clay, "On the Expunging Resolutions," 2:350–54; Anson Burlingame, "Massachusetts and Sumner," 3:13–37; Ignatius Donnelly, "Reconstruction," 4:197–213; William Lloyd Garrison, "Words of Encouragement to the Oppressed," 5:103–15; and a marvelously antic spoof of the sentimental style that was delivered in the U.S. House of Representatives, James Proctor Knott, "Duluth," 6:308–27.

6. Alexis de Tocqueville, *Democracy in America*, part 2, book 1, chaps. 18 and 21.

7. A review of some of these historians can be found in Robert William Fogel and Stanley L. Engerman, *Time on the Cross* (Boston: Little, Brown & Co., 1974), pp. 86–102.

8. Hesketh Pearson, *The Life of Oscar Wilde* (London: Methuen & Co., 1954), pp. 305–7; Frank Harris, *Oscar Wilde: His Life and Confessions* (New York: Horizon Press, 1974), pp. 292–305.

9. Wilde's most magisterial biographer alludes to the perspective that is being proposed here: "Essentially Wilde was conducting, in the most civilized way, an anatomy of his society, and a radical re-

consideration of its ethics. He knew all the secrets and could expose all the pretense." Richard Ellmann, *Oscar Wilde* (New York: Vintage Books, 1988), p. xvi. Wilde himself seems, in the end, to have been moving toward a rhetorical interpretation of his own career: "I was a man who stood in symbolic relations to the art and culture of my age." "De Profundis," in *De Profundis and Other Writings* (Middlesex: Penguin English Library, 1973), p. 151; and again, in almost the same words, ibid., p. 161.

10. The discursive style seems currently unfashionable, but its epistemic function of reflexive censorship has been taken up by other media. The extravagant artistic activities of nazism are worth remembering, as is the pervasive "ignorance" among Germans of what was happening in the concentration camps. In 1936, Walter Benjamin concluded his essay "The Work of Art in the Age of Mechanical Reproduction" with the observation that "fascism is rendering [politics] aesthetic. Communism responds by politicizing art." *Illuminations,* ed. Hannah Arendt, trans. Harry Zohn (New York: Schocken Books, 1969), p. 242.

11. Michael Booth, ed., *Hiss the Villain: Six English and American Melodramas* (London: Eyre and Spottiswoode, 1964). Booth's introduction to this collection (pp. 9–40) is an exceptionally informative analysis of melodrama. A thorough historical treatment of the genre is Frank Rohill's *The World of Melodrama* (University Park: Pennsylvania State University Press, 1967).

Chapter 5. Authoritarian Fiction.

1. Jane Tompkins, Afterword to *The Wide, Wide World* (New York: Feminist Press, City University of New York, 1987), p. 585. All references to the novel will be to this edition.

2. Ibid., p. 584.

3. A sustained consideration of Tompkins's literary criticism of this novel is to be found in D. G. Myers, "The Canonization of Susan Warner," *New Criterion,* December 1988, pp. 73–78.

4. For an account of the links between these therapies and popular religion, see: Catherine L. Albanese, "Physic and Metaphysic in Nineteenth-Century America: Medical Sectarians and Religious Healing," *Church History* 55 (December 1986): 489–502.

5. Esther Menaker provides a summary of Rank's contribution: "He was the first to shift the emphasis in the psychoanalytic understanding of human development from the male-oriented, Oedipal situation of childhood, with its ensuing castration anxiety as the center of conflict, to the initial mother-child relationship." *Otto Rank: A*

Rediscovered Legacy (New York: Columbia University Press, 1982), p. 67.

6. On the evidence that titles in literary anthologies, and hence literary reputations, changed between 1919 and 1962, Jane Tompkins argues against the proposition that "literary values are . . . demonstrably present in certain masterworks." The relationship between claim and warrant in her argument is baffling. See her " 'But Is It Any Good?': The Institutionalization of Literary Value," in *Sensational Designs: The Cultural Work of American Fiction, 1790–1860* (New York: Oxford University Press, 1985), pp. 186–201, esp. pp. 195–96.

7. Jane Tompkins, in her afterword, p. 594, has her own account of the sense of constriction conveyed by the novel: " 'Sentimental' novels take place, metaphorically and literally, in the 'closet.' Their heroines rarely get beyond the confines of a private space—the kitchen, the parlor, the upstairs chamber—and most of what they do takes place inside the 'closet' of the heart. For what the word 'sentimental' means as applied to these novels is that the arena of human action . . . has been defined not as the world but as the human heart. This fiction shares with the reform movement a belief that all true action is not material but spiritual, that one obtains spiritual power through prayer, and that those who know how, in the privacy of their closets, to struggle for possession of their souls will one day possess the world through the power given to them by God. This theory of power makes itself felt, in the mid-nineteenth century, not simply in the explicit assertions of religious propaganda, nor in personal declarations of faith, but as a principle of interpretation that gave form to experience itself."

Elsewhere Tompkins has referred to the novel's "claustrophobic atmosphere." See her "The Other American Renaissance," in *Sensational Designs*, p. 177.

8. This hypothetical account is based on Mussolini's repeated practice. See Frank Iezzi, "Benito Mussolini, Crowd Psychologist," *Quarterly Journal of Speech* 45 (April 1959): 168.

Chapter 6. Ideological Justifications

1. In response to an inquiry about the identity of the author(s) of this editorial, Max Frankel, editor of the editorial page of the *New York Times*, replied by letter, dated 1 November 1983. He wrote, "It is our policy not to identify writers of any editorials and the authorship is often collective."

For convenience, the author(s) of the text is referred to in the conventional third-person singular. The same analysis of the text would be advanced no matter what body, or how many, the mind behind it occupied.

2. *New York Times*, 17 July 1977, p. 20.

Chapter 7. Dramatic Form in Rhetorical Transactions

1. Seymour Chatman, "What Novels Can Do That Films Can't (and Vice Versa)," *On Narrative*, ed. W. J. T. Mitchell (Chicago: University of Chicago Press, 1981), p. 118: "A salient property of narrative is double time structuring. That is, all narratives, in whatever medium, combine the time sequence of plot events, the time of the *histoire* ('story-time') with the time of the presentation of those events in the text, which we call 'discourse-time.' What is fundamental to narrative, regardless of medium, is that these two time orders are independent."

Chatman does not conceive of narrative as necessarily entailing a narrator, which may be a useful conception for his purposes, but is not for mine.

2. Richard Nixon, *RN: The Memoirs of Richard Nixon* (New York: Grosset & Dunlap, 1978), p. 410.

3. The speech has been the subject of lively dispute among rhetorical critics. James R. Andrews has collected the essays of the main antagonists in *The Practice of Rhetorical Criticism*, 2d ed. (New York: Longman, 1990), pp. 100–150.

Of the critics in Andrews's collection, Hermann G. Stelzner in "The Quest Story and Nixon's November 3, 1969 Address," pp. 111–20, saw most clearly the remarkably reflexive character of the speech; but his critique is an account of the speech's narrative structure. Narrative criticism seems fixated on the single rhetorical canon of *dispositio*.

4. "Any first-person narrative . . . may prove unreliable because it issues from a speaking or writing self addressing someone. This is the condition of discourse, in which, as we know, the possibility of speaking the truth creates the possibility of misunderstanding, misperceiving, and lying." Wallace Martin, *Recent Theories of Narrative* (Ithaca: Cornell University Press, 1986), p. 142.

5. For a full account of brainwashing procedures and their effects see: William Sargant, *Battle for the Mind: A Physiology of Conversion and Brain-Washing* (Baltimore: Penguin Books, 1961).

6. Irvin J. Rein, "The New England Transcendentalists: Rhetoric of Paradox" (Ph.D. diss., University of Pittsburgh, 1966), esp. pp. 179–82. See also: John H. Sloan, "'The Miraculous Uplifting': Emerson's

Relationship with His Audience," *Quarterly Journal of Speech* 42 (February 1966): 10–15.

7. Cf. "The Mutability of Rhetoric" later in this volume.

8. John Henry Newman had a similar problem in 1864. He solved it with the publication of *Apologia pro vita sua,* which accomplished for him what I am suggesting Nixon did not—probably could not—accomplish for himself.

9. Phillip Wander, "The Rhetoric of American Foreign Policy," *Quarterly Journal of Speech* 70 (February 1984): 351–63. After an illuminating examination of American diplomatic idioms, Wander argues in the last section of his essay that collective terms become dangerous when they refer to other nationals. My present point is that television, as a medium in which foreign affairs are reported, tends to subvert such consolidations. As Wander convincingly argues, to make war on people, we must first dehumanize them. Seeing films of their children undermines that process.

10. Gertrude Stein, *Narration: Four Lectures by Gertrude Stein,* with an introduction by Thornton Wilder (Chicago: University of Chicago Press, 1935), p. 31.

11. Ibid., p. 17.

12. Nixon indirectly acknowledged as much in *Memoirs:* "As of December [1973], the opinion polls showed that the people were still undecided. Fifty-four percent were against requiring me to leave office. At the same time, 45 percent would respect me more if I resigned so that the nation could concentrate on other problems than Watergate. The very thing I had been counting on to work in my favor had begun to work against me. In April 1973 I had hoped that the public would get tired of Watergate and apply pressure to Congress and the media to move on to other things. But the congressional and media assault and the controversy over the White House tapes had so embroiled me in Watergate that the public was increasingly seeing me as the roadblock and their desire to move on to other things was affecting their willingness to have me removed. Unless I could do something to stem this tide, it would sweep me out of office" (p. 972).

13. In "Pat Loud: An Interview by Melinda Ward," *Film Comment* (20 November 1973), Pat Loud was quoted as saying: "There were lots of things about us that they could have praised that would have helped balance it for us emotionally, but they didn't. We were not treated as human beings at all. We were just dissected like a frog on a biology table. It was inhumane; it was people not really understanding what it took to do some of those scenes—how hard it was

for us to do some of those scenes. Nobody cared a hoot about that. They just rushed in to criticize what we did" (p. 23).

14. Reagan's uses of television are illuminated in Kathleen Hall Jamieson, *Eloquence in an Electronic Age: The Transformation of Political Speechmaking* (New York: Oxford University Press, 1988).

Chapter 8. The Mutability of Rhetoric

1. Paul de Man, *Blindness and Insight: Essays in the Rhetoric of Contemporary Criticism* (New York: Oxford University Press, 1971), p. 37.

2. "Beneath the great continuities of thought, beneath the solid, homogeneous manifestations of a single mind or of a collective mentality, beneath the stubborn development of a science striving to exist and to reach completion at the very outset, beneath the persistence of a particular genre, form, discipline, or theoretical activity, one is now trying to detect the incidence of interruptions. Interruptions whose status and nature vary considerably. There are the *epistemological acts and thresholds* described by Bachelard: they suspend the continuous accumulation of knowledge, interrupt its slow development, and force it to enter a new time, cut it off from its empirical origin and its original motivations, cleanse it of its imaginary complicities; they direct historical analysis away from the search for silent beginnings, and the never-ending tracing-back to the original precursors, towards the search for a new type of rationality and its various effects." Michel Foucault, *The Archeology of Knowledge*, trans. A. M. Sheridan Smith (New York: Harper & Row, 1972), p. 4.

3. Lloyd F. Bitzer, "Aristotle's Enthymeme Revisited," *Quarterly Journal of Speech* 45 (December 1959): esp. 407–8.

4. Aristotle, *Rhetoric* 2.12–18.

5. Aristotle's discussion, in *Rhetoric* 1.8, of the differing forms of government and their differing audiences emphasizes the cohesiveness of each audience and the unitary character of its political convictions. This emphasis is highlighted in such statements as: "All men are ruled by their own interest and their interest lies in whatever preserves the State." *The Rhetoric of Aristotle*, trans. Lane Cooper (New York: Appleton-Century-Crofts, 1932), p. 44. Also, "It is quite necessary to observe the end or aim of each form [of government], for the citizens make their choices with reference to the end. . . . Clearly, then, we must distinguish the tendencies, institutions, and interests which promote the end of each form of government, since *it is with reference to this end that peoples make their choices. . . .* And hence as speakers we should have a command of the character . . .

of each form of government; since for each form its own character
. . . will be most persuasive" (p. 45). Italics added.

6. Erich Kahler, *Man the Measure* (New York: Pantheon, 1943), p.
156.

7. Robert K. Merton, *Mass Persuasion: The Social Psychology of a War
Bond Drive* (New York: Harper & Brothers, 1946), pp. 79–96.

8. Why Greek actors wore masks has been one of the most entertaining puzzles confronted by students of ancient drama. The explanations have been numerous. Let me add another: Maybe they wore
masks because they found it difficult to "put on a face." To pretend
an emotion that one does not feel (*pace* Stanislavsky) requires the
detachment of conviction from behavior that I am suggesting was
rare in the pre-Christian era. Cf. H. D. F. Kitto, *Form and Meaning in
Drama* (London: Methuen, 1956), pp. 218–19, for other explanations
of the mask. Especially relevant to the matter at hand is Kitto's argument that masks suited classical drama because "the drama avoided
purely individual traits and transient moods or emotions."

9. Bruno Snell argued that the very conception of mind or intellect,
while Greek in origin, is post-Homeric. See his *The Discovery of the
Mind: The Greek Origins of European Thought,* trans. T. G. Rosenmeyer
(New York: Harper & Brothers, 1960), esp. pp. v–xi and 1–22.

11. Hegel's interpretation of the trial and death of Socrates is germane to this exploration. Hegel vindicates the Athenian jury on the
grounds that Socrates had subversively affirmed the individuality of
conscience (the daemon) in preference to the communal sources of
moral knowledge (the Delphic oracle, for example). According to
Hegel, the principle that Socrates defended ultimately became "the
ruin of the Athenian people," but one whose development "constitutes the content of all successive history." See *Hegel's Lectures on the
History of Philosophy,* ed. and trans. E. S. Haldane, 3 vols. (London:
Routledge & Kegan Paul, 1955), 1: 426–48. Whatever their philosophical merit, those pages of Hegel must surely be among the most
brilliant displays of exegetical virtuosity ever written.

11. Kahler, *Man the Measure,* p. 174.

12. Friedrich Solmsen, "Greek Ideas about Leisure," *Wingspread
Lectures in the Humanities* (Racine: Johnson Foundation, 1966), pp.
34–35.

13. Snell, *The Discovery of the Mind,* pp. 69, 65.

14. Ian Watt, *The Rise of the Novel* (Berkeley and Los Angeles: University of California Press, 1967), p. 61.

15. "Myth has always been described as the result of an unconscious activity and as a free product of imagination. . . . The new

political myths do not grow up freely; they are not wild fruits of an exuberant imagination. They are artificial things fabricated by very skillful and cunning artisans. It has been reserved for the twentieth century, our own great technical age, to develop a new technique of myth. Henceforth myths can be manufactured in the same sense and according to the same methods as any other modern weapon—as machine guns or airplanes. That is a new thing—and a thing of crucial importance. It has changed the whole form of our social life." Ernst Cassirer, *The Myth of the State* (New Haven: Yale University Press, 1946), p. 282.

16. "The rhetorical function is the *function of adjusting ideas to people and of people to ideas.*" Donald C. Bryant, "Rhetoric: Its Function and Its Scope," *Quarterly Journal of Speech* 39 (December 1953): 413.

Index